# Developmental Coaching

*Developmental Coaching* explores many of the common transition points we experience throughout life, including teenage transitions, becoming a parent, mid-life and retirement. The book sets these transitions in their social context and reviews them in the light of generational factors.

The book is introduced with key psychological concepts from areas such as lifespan development and positive psychology, in addition to insights from other disciplines, including management theory and sociology. The main topics of discussion are:

- coaching tools and techniques
- broader societal and generational trends
- how coaching can help individuals to realise positive growth.

With case studies throughout, *Developmental Coaching* offers an essential resource for practising coaches, coaching psychologists, counsellors and other professionals who wish to further their knowledge of the developmental aspects of coaching and dealing with life transitions.

**Stephen Palmer** PhD is Director and Honorary Professor of Psychology of the Coaching Psychology Unit, at City University London and Founder Director of the Centre for Coaching. He is an APECS Accredited Executive Coach and Supervisor and an award-winning psychologist. He has written or edited 35 books, including the *Handbook of Coaching Psychology* (with Whybrow). He is Honorary President of the Society for Coaching Psychology.

**Sheila Panchal** CPsychol is a Registered Occupational Psychologist. She has applied positive and coaching psychology in a range of organisational settings. She holds a Professional Development Certificate in Coaching Psychology from the University of Sydney, and is Honorary Secretary of the Society for Coaching Psychology.

# Essential Coaching Skills and Knowledge
Series Editors: Gladeana McMahon,
Stephen Palmer & Averil Leimon

The **Essential Coaching Skills and Knowledge** series provides an accessible and lively introduction to key areas in the developing field of coaching. Each title in the series is written by leading coaches with extensive experience and has a strong practical emphasis, including illustrative vignettes, summary boxes, exercises and activities. Assuming no prior knowledge, these books will appeal to professionals in business, management, human resources, psychology, counselling and psychotherapy, as well as to students and tutors of coaching and coaching psychology.

www.routledgementalhealth.com/essential-coaching-skills

*Titles in the series:*

**Essential Business Coaching**
*Averil Leimon, François Moscovici & Gladeana McMahon*

**Achieving Excellence in Your Coaching Practice:
How to Run a Highly Successful Coaching Business**
*Gladeana McMahon, Stephen Palmer & Christine Wilding*

**A Guide to Coaching and Mental Health: The Recognition
and Management of Psychological Issues**
*Andrew Buckley & Carole Buckley*

**Essential Life Coaching Skills**
*Angela Dunbar*

**The Coaching Relationship: Putting People First**
*Stephen Palmer & Almuth McDowall*

**101 Coaching Strategies and Techniques**
*Edited by Gladeana McMahon & Anne Archer*

**Group and Team Coaching: The Essential Guide**
*Christine Thornton*

**Coaching Women to Lead**
*Averil Leimon, François Moscovici & Helen Goodier*

**Developmental Coaching: Life Transitions and
Generational Perspectives**
*Edited by Stephen Palmer & Sheila Panchal*

# Developmental Coaching

## Life Transitions and Generational Perspectives

*Edited by Stephen Palmer
and Sheila Panchal*

Routledge
Taylor & Francis Group

LONDON AND NEW YORK

First published 2011
by Routledge
27 Church Road, Hove, East Sussex BN3 2FA

Simultaneously published in the USA and Canada
by Routledge
270 Madison Avenue, New York NY 10016

*Routledge is an imprint of the Taylor & Francis Group, an Informa business*

Typeset in New Century Schoolbook by
RefineCatch Limited, Bungay, Suffolk
Printed and bound in Great Britain by
TJ International Ltd, Padstow, Cornwall
Paperback cover design Lisa Dynan

*British Library Cataloguing in Publication Data*
A catalogue record for this book is available from the British Library

*Library of Congress Cataloging-in-Publication Data*
Developmental coaching : life transitions and generational perspectives/
edited by Stephen Palmer and Sheila Panchal.
    p. cm.
Includes index.
ISBN 978–0–415–47359–0 (hbk.) – ISBN 978–0–415–47360–6 (pbk.)
1. Personal coaching. 2. Aging–Psychological aspects.
3. Age groups–Psychological aspects. 4. Change (Psychology)
I. Palmer, Stephen, 1955- II. Panchal, Sheila.
    BF637.P36D48 2010
    158'.3—dc22

                                    2010017476


ISBN: 978–0–415–47359–0 (hbk)
ISBN: 978–0–415–47360–6 (pbk)

# Contents

# Dedications

For my father, and his contribution to my journey.

For Norah, my aunt and godmother, in her ninetieth year. During her lifetime she has lived through many transitions.

And for Aniket, who has just started out on life's journey.

*Stephen*

For my family:
Alexander, Carina and Aaron Kelly,
Sharda, Shashi, Chandrika and Sunil Panchal.

*Sheila*

# About the editors

**Professor Stephen Palmer** is a Chartered Psychologist, an APECS Accredited Executive Coach and Supervisor, an AREBT Accredited Cognitive Behavioural Coach and an SCP accredited Coaching Psychologist. He is Director of the Coaching Psychology Unit at City University and Founder Director of the Centre for Coaching, London. He is Honorary President of the Society for Coaching Psychology and former Honorary President of the Association for Coaching. He has written or edited 35 books, including the *Handbook of Coaching Psychology: A Guide for Practitioners* (with Whybrow, 2007) and *The Coaching Relationship: Putting People First* (with McDowall, 2010). In 2008 the British Psychological Society Special Group in Coaching Psychology gave him the 'Lifetime Achievement Award in Recognition of Distinguished Contribution to Coaching Psychology', awarded at the 1st European Coaching Psychology Conference, 2008.

**Sheila Panchal** is a Chartered Psychologist and Registered Occupational Psychologist. She is co-author of *Turning 30: How to Get the Life You Really Want* (with Jackson, 2005). She has applied positive and coaching psychology in a range of organisational settings. She holds a Professional Development Certificate in Coaching Psychology from the University of Sydney, and is Honorary Secretary of the Society for Coaching Psychology. Sheila specialises in transitions, from developmental turning points to dealing with the stress of organisational change, and has contributed to conferences and publications on these topics.

# Contributors

**Robert Biswas-Diener** is widely known as the 'Indiana Jones of Positive Psychology' because his scientific pursuit of the emotional good life has led him to such far-flung places as India, Greenland, Israel and Kenya. He holds a Master's in Clinical Psychology and is a Certified MentorCoach.

**Emma Donaldson-Feilder** is a Chartered Psychologist and Registered Occupational Psychologist who specialises in helping organisations to achieve sustainable business performance through improvements in the well-being and engagement of staff. She combines research and practitioner roles with writing and presenting on workplace well-being.

**Jenny Fox Eades** is Director of the Celebrating Strengths Programme. Jenny trained as a special needs teacher, has qualifications in counselling and group therapy and has a Master's in Psychoanalytic Observational Studies. She studied with Martin Seligman and is a founder member of Positive Workplace International.

**Ben Green** is a Principal Consultant at Chandler Macleod Consulting in Perth, Australia. As a Chartered Psychologist and Registered Occupational Psychologist he specialises in talent management through objective assessment of behaviour in the workplace. Ben has a particular interest in the cross-cultural and cross-generational aspects of human behaviour.

**P. Alex Linley** is a leading authority on the applications of strengths psychology to organisational development and people practices. He holds the position of Visiting Professor in Psychology at the University of Leicester and has written, co-written or edited more than 100 research papers and book chapters and six books.

**Jennifer Liston-Smith** has 20 years' consultancy and coaching experience in globally known organisations, an Oxford Law degree and a Master's in Psychology. A UK pioneer of corporate maternity coaching, Jennifer is Head of Coaching Development with My Family Care. She also trains and supervises coaches, and contributes through media, professional bodies and conference speaking.

**Siobhain O'Riordan** is a trainer, examiner and supervisor on graduate/postgraduate coaching and coaching psychology programmes. She is an Honorary Research Fellow at City University London and Deputy Director of their Coaching Psychology Unit. She is Editor of *The Coaching Psychologist* and *Coaching Psychology International* and Chair of the Society for Coaching Psychology.

**Angela Puri** has a Psychology degree and a Master's in Occupational and Organisational Psychology. She is a Corporate Equalities and Diversity Officer in the Royal Borough of Kensington and Chelsea (RBKC) and an Honorary Research Fellow at the Centre for Coaching. She is also a co-author of the book *Coping with Stress at University: A Survival Guide* (with Palmer).

**Emma Trenier** works as a Consulting Psychologist and leads the Centre for Applied Positive Psychology's outplacement work. She is passionate about enabling individuals and teams to understand their strengths and how they can use them more.

**Helen Williams** is a Chartered Psychologist and Registered Occupational Psychologist specialising in management development. Previously with SHL, global leader in assessment and development, and now as an independent coaching psychologist, her work involves psychometric assessment and feedback, performance coaching and cognitive-behavioural coaching, facilitation of peer coaching groups and delivery of behavioural change workshops.

# Preface

From international research and practitioner perspectives, coaching and coaching psychology are both continually growing and evolving applied fields. Over the years there has been the increasing emergence of research providing evidence to support coaching effectiveness, as well as the integration of new theories and models. Coaches now work in a variety of settings, with a range of populations and with individuals, groups and organisations. The diversity and breadth of the field are testament to the versatility and effectiveness of the coaching profession.

This book aims to recognise that as coaches and coaching psychologists we are working with individuals across the lifespan, often to support and facilitate them in dealing with transitional periods. Developmental psychology plays a central role in the assumptions and approaches discussed here. In particular, we focus on lifespan transitions, on the journey from childhood to old age, and consider both the specific and connected nature of these points in our lives. We also explore the socio-cultural context for experiencing life transitions, considering generational factors and often drawing on allied disciplines such as sociology and management theory to understand the broader influences on individual experience. Positive psychology is a key influence that has informed this book. It can enable individuals to realise the opportunities for growth that life transitions can offer by focusing on their strengths through coaching and tackling difficult, although often exciting, challenges.

Whilst we emphasise the importance of avoiding stereotypes and assumptions, and respecting individual differences, we believe that coaches, coaching psychologists, mentors and other professionals can draw valuable insights from developmental and generational perspectives to enhance their work. The chapters explore various life transitions, considering both theoretical influences and pragmatic considerations for coaches. Broader themes of positive psychology coaching for transitions and working across generations within organisational settings are also reviewed.

We would like to thank all our authors for sharing their valuable expertise and insights in this book. We hope that this book will inform professional practice and raise many further questions and avenues for exploration.

*Stephen Palmer*
*Sheila Panchal*

# Foreword

That we live in an era of ever-more personal and social turbu-
lence, with ever-fewer social norms and guidelines to show
us the way, is a truism that has never been more apt. This is
perhaps one reason why the coaching profession has been
such a growth industry in recent years. We are not, however,
the first generation to experience the unfreezing of rigid
timetables in the organisation of life events. Nor are we the
first to feel at the mercy of uncertainty and lack of stability.
It was over 30 years ago that Neugarten and Hagestad (1976)
talked of the emergence of the 'fluid life cycle', one marked
by an increasing number of transitions, the disappearance
of traditional timetables for the ordering of life events and a
lack of synchrony among age-related roles. From the standpoint of 2010, it is easy to comment that they could have had
little idea of what was yet to come. Life-cycle fluidity, varia-
tion, instability and uncertainty have all increased significantly in the ensuing decades. We are now in an era where
life stages identified by shared tasks and transitions are, at
least in terms of the years beyond puberty, largely fictitious
– they rarely represent anybody's reality.

And yet, age and life stage have not disappeared as key
dimensions along which we order life experiences. It can be
hard to conjure up a clear image of someone if we do not
know their age. Age hints at some of the formative social,
economic and political events that the person has lived
through. Knowing a person's age can tell us whether they
were born during a time of boom or bust, and whether they
are likely to remember where they were when they learned

that President Kennedy had been shot, that Princess Diana had died or that New York's Twin Towers had collapsed. It will tell us whether they were a child of the Thatcher era or part of the Second World War's 'make do and mend' generation. A person's age will suggest what type of primary school education they have received and the occupational opportunities likely to have been open to them when they reached school-leaving age.

Whilst to draw attention to age may smack of ageism, it would be ridiculous to suggest that being 25 years old is the same as being 75 years old. And whilst it has become ever-more hazardous to predict the timing, or even occurrence, of key life events such as marriage, parenthood, graduation or retirement, the point in the life course at which these events do occur can be significant. Pregnancy at age 15 years, for example, is not the same as pregnancy at age 45 years; nor is redundancy at age 27 years the same as redundancy at age 57 years. Furthermore, age is used, albeit inconsistently, as a benchmark for allocating rights and responsibilities throughout society and as a gatekeeper guarding access to services. Many services – including those offered by life coaches – are defined directly or indirectly by clients' age or life stage.

To ignore age (or at least to try to) is to ignore an important dimension of difference and potentially to devalue the experiences with which a life has been filled. 'While difference is celebrated in axes such as race, gender, religion and nationality,' writes Andrews (1999), 'the same is not true for age. . . . (And yet) years are not empty containers: important things happen in that time. Why must these years be trivialised? They are the stuff of which people's lives are made' (p. 309). Andrews (2000) uses the term 'agefulness' to capture the idea of a life filled with accumulated experience. The challenge is to acknowledge this whilst at the same time avoiding the construction of a set of age-based stereotypes that form a cultural straitjacket into which we are forced or feel obliged to squeeze ourselves.

Coaching has always adopted a developmental stance – if sometimes only implicitly. It looks forward rather than backwards and is less concerned with restitution and more with prospective work to forestall future misdirection or stagnation. *Developmental Coaching: Life Transitions and Generational Perspectives* makes this affinity explicit, and when it links coaching with positive psychology and places it within a life-course and transition context it offers a timely new slant on coaching practice. There is rapport between the values of positive psychology and coaching – an emphasis on solutions, for example, on strengths, on clear and explicit goals and strategies. Both are adherents of 'glass-half-full' rather than 'glass-half-empty' thinking. To set these well-matched stable companions in the context of life-course and transition theory is a master stroke.

Both lifespan developmental psychology and transition theory grapple with tensions between change and continuity, with the significance of the timing of life events and, perhaps most significantly in the present context, the balance between gain and loss. Transition theory posits that we are attached by affectional bonds (Parkes, 1971) to the elements within our life space and that these bonds, by definition, resist severance – if only via the 'better the devil you know' line of argument. As all change involves the severance or, at the very least, loosening and renegotiation of affectional bonds then, also by definition, all change requires that we deal with the prospect of loss. This realisation rescues both coaching and positive psychology from accusations of over-optimism and a tendency to turn their back on the realities of the constraints of many people's opportunity structures.

*Developmental Coaching: Life Transitions and Generational Perspectives* reflects a broadening of perspective by the coaching profession. It represents a drawing back of the camera to embrace more of the wider context in which the practice of coaching takes place. It embeds specific transitions and transitional periods not only within the total life course, but also within their specific social, cultural and historical context. And throughout all of this, it shows how questions of identity – 'Who am I?', 'Who was I?' and 'Who am I to become?' – echo down the years.

*Dr Léonie Sugarman*
*University of Cumbria*
*September 2010*

# References

Andrews, M. (1999) The seductiveness of agelessness. *Aging and Society, 19*: 301–318.

Andrews, M. (2000) Ageful and proud. *Aging and Society, 20*: 791–795.

Neugarten, B. L., and Hagestad, G. O. (1976) Age and the life course. In R. H. Binstock and E. Shanas (Eds.), *Handbook of Aging and the Social Sciences* (pp. 35–55). New York: Van Nostrand Reinhold.

Parkes, C. M. (1971) Psycho-social transitions: A field for study. *Social Science and Medicine, 5*: 101–105.

# Life transitions and generational perspectives

## *Stephen Palmer and Sheila Panchal*

*He who has a why to live can bear with almost any how*
(Friedrich Nietzsche, quoted in Frankl, 1963: 121)

Much has been written about coaching and coaching psychology practice, advocating a range of theories, models and views to enhance coach effectiveness. This book considers the 'big picture' and offers perspectives that provide relevant context for coaches working with individuals in a variety of settings.

This chapter will start by considering the emerging field of 'developmental coaching' and the range of approaches that exist within it. Then we will focus on our particular definition of 'developmental coaching' and review relevant theory and generational perspectives that relate to it. The specific book chapters will then be reviewed and, finally, an integrated model presented that builds on commonalities and linkages between transitions.

## 'Developmental coaching'

'Developmental coaching' is an emerging and rapidly growing field. It could be argued that all coaching is developmental in some respect, yet some researchers are using the term 'developmental' to emphasise particular aspects of coaching. One angle focuses on a holistic perspective that stretches beyond skills or performance coaching to encompass the growth of the 'whole person'. For example, in the context of the workplace, Leonard-Cross (2010: 36) offers the following description:

Developmental coaching describes coaching that addresses the whole person. Being holistic in nature, it can involve home and work life, plus more personal professional issues (Grant and Cavanagh, 2004) such as relationship and career issues. It is essentially non-directive as the coach assumes the role of facilitator, primarily listening and asking questions and acting as a 'thought partner'. This is also the type of coaching preferred by most coachees (Bacon, 2003).

Cox and Jackson (2010) offer an extensive review of the existing 'developmental coaching' literature. They also recognise it to be 'a natural progression from skills and performance coaching' (217) to a focus on 'the growth of the person to be all that he/she can be' (218). They note the breadth and complexity of the topic and acknowledge the different types of adult development theories that have been drawn upon, namely physical development, intellectual or cognitive development and lifespan development theories. In particular, cognitive-developmental theories (e.g. Piaget, 1972; Kegan, 1982, 1994; Loevinger, 1976) have been applied to coaching (see Bachirova, 2010; Bachirova and Cox, 2007). Key researchers in this area have placed emphasis on understanding the developmental stage and capabilities of the coach as well as coachee, and using this perspective to explore the coach–coacheee relationship more fully (see Laske, 2008: 125). Alongside such constructivist-developmental approaches, Cox and Jackson (2010) also point to the influence of other theoretical traditions in the 'developmental coaching' field, notably person-centred, cognitive-behavioural and narrative approaches.

Problems exist with the existing theories (largely untested) and even with definitions of development. Adult development theory is informed by a number of theories that still need further research (see Knowles, Holton and Swanson, 2005) and to compound this problem the terms 'development' and 'developmental' are not clear either (Sugarman, 2001: 3):

> Not all change across the life course would necessarily be described as developmental. 'Development' is not an empirical term (Reese and Overton, 1970), although on occasions it is used as though it were (Kaplan, 1983). No

matter how much data we're able to collect about the course of an individual's life this, of itself, would not enable us to define what is meant by the term 'development', unless, that is, we were to say that whatever happens across the life span is what constitutes development. This, however, would reduce developmental psychology to a largely atheoretical data-collection exercise.

Cox and Jackson (2010: 219) state:

> It could be argued that it is impossible to fully capture the considerable complexity of the tasks and processes involved in adult development. As Kolb (1984: 138) notes, 'The paths of development can be as varied as the many systems of social knowledge'. By extension, we would argue that any particular model of development is a partial perspective and cannot reflect the range of developmental opportunities evident in coaching practice.

Many publications regarding the theory and research of lifespan development have focused on areas such as counselling and therapy (e.g. Sugarman, 1996, 2010; Sugarman and Wolfe, 1989; Thomas, 1990), whereas the growing field of 'developmental coaching' examines how similar developmental perspectives can be useful for coaches.

## *Transitions, generations and growth*

The view of 'developmental coaching' that is explored in this book encompasses three key facets: life transitions, generational perspectives and positive growth. It is complementary to the aforementioned conceptualisations of 'developmental coaching', yet adopts a somewhat different slant by specifically focusing on the developmental potential of key transition points across the lifespan. It explores some of the implications of ageing, yet recognises that despite the inevitability of ageing, people develop differently.

Our approach is largely informed by lifespan development theory and concentrates on the transitional aspects suggested by such theory. The concepts of 'transition' and 'crisis' are central to the views of theorists such as Erikson (1950) and Levinson (1986), and form the basis of discussions in this book. By life transitions we mean key turning points that many of us are likely to experience during the lifespan, with varying degrees of opportunity and challenge. Although life transitions can include specific events such as moving job or house, this book considers more global, life transitions, such as mid-life and becoming a parent. Levinson (1986: 7) conceptualises adult development as consisting of alternating stable (6–10 years) and transitional (4–5 years) periods:

> The primary tasks of every transition period are to question and reappraise the existing structure, to explore the various possibilities for change in self and world, and to move toward a commitment to crucial choices that form a basis for a new life structure in the ensuing stable period.

Life transitions can be considered as opportunities for learning and development (e.g. Merriam, 1998), and our definition of 'developmental coaching' relates to how coaches support individuals to negotiate transitions, and therefore grow and develop. As with all coaching, it involves greater self-awareness and accountability. Specific to 'developmental coaching' is the idea that there may be challenges associated with a particular stage, or phase, of life that need to be addressed. This is in line with Garvey (2009), who also considers coaching in the context of age transitions and generations.

The second key concept associated with 'developmental coaching' is that of the broader social context and generational factors. By this we mean having a view of cultural and generational trends that may influence an individual's experience of life transitions. For example, in what ways does mid-life differ today from 50 years ago? What demographic and cultural trends influence the opportunities and challenges people are faced with this during this time of life? Having an awareness of these 'big picture' trends can set the context for effective 'developmental coaching'. For example, Strenger and Ruttenberg's (2008) research sets mid-life in context by pointing to increased life expectancy and the changing job market as key factors that have enhanced the potential for today's mid-lifers to have second lives and careers.

Finally, a central assumption associated with 'developmental coaching' is to facilitate a positive stance towards growing older, consistent with work on 'positive ageing' and positive psychology in general. This allows individuals to focus on their strengths and take advantage of the developmental and transformational opportunities associated with each transition rather than become mired with anxiety or concern. Levy and associates (2002) noted a link between positive self-perceptions of ageing and longevity. Strenger and Ruttenberg (2008) highlighted that the notion of 'mid-life change' and associated opportunities is in fact more prevalent than the trauma of mid-life crisis (Jacques, 1965). For comprehensive reviews of the alignment of positive psychology and coaching, see Linley and Harrington (2010), and Kauffman, Boniwell and Silberman (2010).

To summarise, our definition is:

*Developmental coaching facilitates the effective negotiation of key lifespan transitions, supporting positive growth and development. It draws insight from the relevant broader context influencing the coachee experience of transition, such as social and cultural factors and generational influences.*

Clearly, it is important throughout to remember individual differences and avoid limiting stereotypes and labels. Not all teenagers experience the same 'angst', and not all Baby Boomers share the same characteristics. The chapters share both theoretical perspectives and practical experiences that may bring some broader insight into the coaching process.

## Key theories

A wide range of theory and research is discussed in the book, drawing on many areas of psychology and introducing insights from other allied disciplines such as anthropology, sociology and management theory. Running throughout the book is a focus on lifespan development theory; key theorists include Erikson (1950, 1995) and Levinson (1986), who describe adult development in terms of phases or stages. For example, psychoanalyst Erikson outlines eight stages and notes specific conflicts associated with each that serve as turning points for development. The idea is that each step builds on skills learned previously:

1 **Infant (0–18 months): Basic trust versus mistrust**. This depends on how reliable the child perceives their caregiver to be. If the child is able to trust them, they have the basis for security. If a child is cared for by people who are inconsistent, rejecting or emotionally unavailable, they will be fearful and mistrusting of the world.

2 **Toddler (18 months–3 years): Autonomy versus shame/doubt**. The child is engaged with gaining greater control of tasks such as bodily functions and a selection of activities. If successful, they develop confidence and autonomy, but if not they can be left with a sense of doubt and inadequacy.

3 **Pre-school (3–5 years): Initiative versus guilt**. The child continues to make choices and assert control over others through play. A sense of initiative and mastery is the outcome of this stage, or guilt through disapproval if the child exerts too much control.

4 **School years (6–11 years): Industry versus inferiority**. Within school settings, children are able to compare themselves to others. Ideally, they should develop pride in their academic and social skills, because without this they can feel inferior and doubting.

5 **Adolescence (12–18 years): Identity versus confusion**. The task of adolescence is to explore the world and develop a sense of self. Those who are less successful can feel confused about who they are and how they fit into the world.

6 **Young adulthood (19–40 years): Intimacy versus isolation**. The focus now is on intimate relationships and the ability to develop secure, committed relationships. It can also concern commitments to career and family. Those unable to commit can feel alone in life.

7 **Middle age (40–65 years): Generativity versus self-absorption and stagnation**. Adults continue to build careers and families, and contribute to future generations in some way. Those who are unsuccessful can experience life as unproductive and unsatisfying.
8 **Maturity (65–death): Ego integrity versus despair**. As individuals face the end of their lives, they tend to reflect back and feel either satisfied with their achievements or bitter and regretful.

Theories such as Erikson's highlight the similarities and universalities within the life cycle, yet have been criticised for ignoring the complexity and individuality of adult development. It is important to acknowledge that each individual is unique and has a particular set of experiences that influence their personality, identity and path. Hendry and Kloep (2002) talk about a dynamic lifelong process of accumulating and losing resources that is different for every individual. Also of note is the concept of continuity across the lifespan as opposed to discrete stages.

The perspectives offered in this book also aim to contextualise life stages by discussing social and cultural factors that determine how the conflicts, challenges and opportunities may be experienced in our current social setting.

Theories of self are relevant for coaches supporting individuals through life transitions. For example, Markus and Nurius (1986: 954) posited a cognitive theory of self by asserting that all individuals have a range of 'possible selves' – the people we would like to become, expect to become, or fear becoming:

> Possible selves are the ideal selves that we would very much like to become. They are also the selves that we could become and are afraid of becoming. The possible selves that are hoped for might include the successful self, the creative self, the rich self, the thin self, or the loved and admired self, whereas, the dreaded possible selves could be the alone self, the depressed self, the incompetent self, the alcoholic self, the unemployed self, or the bag lady self.

This concept can be explored with coachees. Are their possible selves aspirational or feared? How can they move towards the aspired self? As life progresses, is there a sense that time is running out to move towards those aspired selves, and is there more potential for anxiety associated with feared selves?

When considering transitions in particular, useful insights can be gained from transition psychology. This was seminally researched by Elisabeth Kubler-Ross (1969), based on experiences of illness and bereavement, and has been followed by similar theories (e.g. Bridges, 1995). These theories indicate that transitions can be times of both challenge and opportunity and can bring forth a range of emotions, from despair to excitement. All changes involve loss and letting go, living with ambiguity and the possibilities of new beginnings. While this is a useful model, often discussed in relation to specific changes such as redundancy or moving house, it is also helpful when considering broader life transitions such as retirement and mid-life. Coachees can benefit from realising that much of the uncertainty and varied emotion they are experiencing is a 'normal' aspect of experiencing transition, change and ultimately growth.

Holmes and Rahe (1967) created the Social Readjustment Rating Scale, a scale of stressful life events that provides another useful perspective on significant life transitions. Top of the list are death of a spouse, divorce and marital separation. A similar scale has also been developed for non-adults, which notes marriage, unwed pregnancy and death of a parent as the top three most stressful events. Life stages, especially when many of these events are likely to cluster, can be particularly stressful. For example, divorce is more likely at mid-life than other periods. As a coach, it can be helpful to consider the types of life events that an individual is experiencing and their impact. Clearly, they need to be contextualised – unwed pregnancy may have been more stress-inducing 50 years ago than today due to the norms and conventions of the time.

Stress and coping perspectives provide additional insight (e.g. Palmer and Cooper, 2010; Palmer and Gyllensten,

2010). Acknowledging that transition can be a stressful time, one role of the coach is to build coping strategies and resources in individuals. These can range from challenging thinking styles to physical exercise. Such strategies can be applied from one transition to another: For example, if a teenager learns how to maximise the benefits of social support and 'ask for help' during these years, they can draw on these skills when negotiating later transitions, such as 'turning 30'. Schlossberg, Waters and Goodman's (1995) transition theory identifies four sets of factors that influence a person's ability to cope with transition – situation, self, support and strategies. At the extreme, transitions can be the catalyst for severe anxiety and depression. Stanley and associates (2009) suggested that transition is a useful concept when considering risk factors for suicide. They studied student suicide in higher education, based on 20 case studies.

Carl Jung, a Swiss psychiatrist and psychotherapist, noted the process of individuation that occurs throughout life but comes to the fore in the second half as we become more consciously aware of ourselves and our strengths and the need to face or deal with our limitations (see Jung and De Laszlo, 1958, 1959). The coach may observe that a coachee has a lack of self-confidence as they drift into a mid-life crisis, with possibly a temporary loss of meaning in their life and a need for career or personal coaching.

A key theoretical underpinning for much of this book is positive psychology (e.g. Seligman, 2003). Chapter 8 is devoted to positive psychology and strengths coaching through transition; other chapters draw heavily on theory and practice when considering the various life transitions. With transitions, as with all types of coaching, a wide range of coaching theories and approaches can be applied, which are also discussed throughout the book. Particular emphasis is placed on positive psychology as it can support two strands within 'developmental coaching'. One is that of acting as a coping resource – building skills such as gratitude, optimism and savouring pleasure as ways of increasing positive emotion into daily life and therefore making the task of transition easier. For example, Seligman and associates

(2005) found that for depressed individuals writing down 'three good things' daily and 'using signature strengths in a new way' increased happiness and reduced depressive symptoms for six months. The second is to actually support the self-awareness and decision-making associated with the transition: for example, identifying strengths can help to answer the question 'who am I?'; and asking questions about meaning and purpose focus on 'what is my place in the world?', a key aspect associated with negotiating life transitions and facilitating positive development.

Sugarman (1986) summarises two main perspectives associated with life events or transitions. The 'disease' model views these as stressful, or 'crises', so the aim of intervention is therefore to avoid, eliminate or reduce stress so that an individual can continue with 'normal' development. By contrast, the 'developmental' approach considers transitions as states of imbalance that precede and enable growth. Intervention goals therefore focus on how the individual can learn and develop as a result of a transition or life event, as is the case with 'developmental coaching'.

## Generational factors

Within the book, various generations will be discussed. This aims to provide insight into how broader social factors can affect the way in which life transitions are experienced today. Generational definitions vary, but broadly speaking they fall into the following categories (adapted from CIPD, 2008):

- *Veterans* (or Traditionalists), born 1939–1947. Experienced World War II during their childhood.
- *Baby Boomers*, born 1948–1963. Grew up in a time of social change, including a push for civil rights and the women's movement.
- *Generation X*, born 1964–1978. Early Gen X would have experienced the recession of the early 1980s. Later Gen X would have experienced increasing commercialism.
- *Generation Y* (or Millennials), born 1979–1991. Primarily the children of Baby Boomers, Gen Y grew up in a time of relative peace and posterity, other than terrorism and the

latest recession. Heavily influenced by the rapid change in technology,

* *Generation Z*, born 1991–2010. Technology is an even greater influence. Most have never known life without the internet and mobile phones. Terrorism and climate change are real concerns, as is the latest recession.
* *Generation A/Alpha*, born 2010+. First truly millennial generation, entirely born in the 21st century. As children of Generation Y, they are born to parents stressed by recession.

There are clear cross-cultural differences within these categories. The definitions above reference broad trends and events within developed Western societies and should be considered within this context.

Transcending all generations are some broad social themes that influence how we live today. Our view of 'developmental coaching' keeps these influences in mind as useful context when coaching individuals. Of course, there are many other potential environmental influences, such as specific familial or organisational factors:

* **Consumerism** and materialism is a significant influence in today's Western societies, associated with celebrity culture and mass advertising. For example, the average child in the UK, USA and Australia sees between 20,000 and 40,000 TV commercials per year (from Palmer, 2006). Seligman and associates (1995) talk about the changes that have taken place in the lifetime of Baby Boomers, noting that society has transformed from an achievement-oriented society to a feel-good society. According to Seligman and associates (1995), the impact of an individualist, consumer-oriented society deprives people of the satisfaction associated with achieving goals and experiencing meaning through activities and communities larger than themselves. As such, it could be associated with depression. This view is echoed by James (2007), who in his book entitled *Affluenza* associated higher rates of mental illness in consumerist nations with excessive wealth-seeking. This concept was introduced by Fromm (1976), who argued that two ways of existence were competing for 'the spirit of mankind' – having and being.

The having mode looks to things and material possessions and is based on aggression and greed. The being mode is rooted in love and is concerned with shared experience and productive activity. With this in mind, tackling questions of meaning could be more problematic for those living in today's consumerist society, across all generations. As a result, a significant role of the coach may be to explore what is truly meaningful for an individual, and how this changes over time.

- **Social mobility**. Today's society is more global, mobile and transient than previously, with people living in different locations and travelling frequently within or between countries. Dynamics of societies and organisations are changing to reflect these trends. This broad change creates opportunities not available in the past, such as experiencing a range of cultures and greater potential for career growth. Challenges include more transient communities, which can affect social support and promote new challenges for relationships. For example, many new parents now do not have the guidance of their own parents and close friends.

- **Technology**. Already mentioned as a particularly strong driver for Generations Y, Z and A/Alpha, advances in technology affect experiences across the board. The internet means that information is available in an instant, at our fingertips, and our ability to connect with others via non-face-to-face means is extensive. The meteoric rise of social networking sites such as Facebook and Twitter demonstrates the power of this trend. Technological progress has opened up significant opportunities for gathering knowledge, communication and flexible working practices. Laptops and blackberries mean that employees are no longer limited to the office. There may also be downsides, in terms of inhibiting relationship building, reducing engagement in physical activity and affecting work–life balance. Perhaps technological advance has led to an 'absence of presence' (M. Palmer, 2010, personal communication).

- **Choice**. Perhaps the overriding social change can be summarised as one of choice. In contrast to 50 years ago, individuals are faced with unprecedented choice and opportunity, facilitated by the previously discussed changes of consumerism, social mobility and technology. When negotiating life transitions these choices can be inspiring and motivating. A young person at school is faced with a wide array of subjects to study. The next step on to university, college or the workplace can involve making both exciting and challenging choices that can have a life-long impact upon the individual. At mid-life, people can consider alternative careers. At retirement, people may consider travel or volunteering. Whilst coaches can help individuals to take advantage of these opportunities, they also need to be mindful of the 'paradox of choice' (Schwartz, 2003). When faced with what may seem like endless choices, individuals can become paralysed and fearful of making the 'wrong' choice. Coaching can play an important role in focusing the individual on personal values and strengths as a basis for decision-making. They can also encourage decision-making strategies associated with 'satisficing' (aiming for 'good enough') rather than 'maximising' (aiming for 'best'). Schwartz and associates (2002) found negative correlations between maximisation and happiness, optimism, self-esteem and life satisfaction. They found that 'maximisers' are more likely to engage in social comparison than 'satisficers' and to experience regret.

Other social trends exist, such as obesity and the economic climate (which at the time of writing this book is in the midst of a significant downturn). For developmental coaches, these trends can influence the way their coachees experience and successfully negotiate life transitions.

Legislative changes are also relevant. For example, in the UK the Age Discrimination Act came into effect in 2006 to tackle age discrimination in organisations. Similar legislation exists in some other European countries, as well as in the USA and Australia. Perhaps even more so than with gender and ethnicity, we are all prone to making assumptions about age. Equally, policy changes can influence transitions around parenthood and retirement. For example, fathers are increasingly involved in childrearing, especially as some European countries, including the UK, open up to longer periods of paternity leave. The recent lifting of retirement age in the UK is another notable change.

Finally, demographic changes, namely increased life expectancy, are of note. The Office for National Statistics (2009) states that UK life expectancy for females is 81.6 years and for males is 77.4 years (based on 2006–2008 data). This has increased considerably in the last century; the figures were 49 and 45 years, respectively, in 1901 (House of Commons, 1999). This has implications for numerous transitions. For example, people could now be spending 20+ years post-retirement. Early adulthood is experienced as an extended adolescence and '30 becomes the new 20'. Journalist Gail Sheehy described commonly experienced life stages in her book entitled *Passages* in 1976. In 1995 she published an updated version, *New Passages*, which noted that people are taking longer to grow up and much longer to die, thus shifting all the stages of adulthood by up to 10 years.

As noted upfront, stereotypes and assumptions are to be avoided. The discussion about broad social trends and generational differences is aimed at highlighting the 'bigger picture' that affects how life transitions may be experienced in today's Western society, and the associated opportunities and pressures. Clearly, we have discussed a snapshot in time, and trends and demographics will continue to shift and evolve. The message to coaches is to stay aware of these broader influences and how they may be affecting the experience of coachees.

## Key transitions

The book chapters offer rich and diverse perspectives, covering a range of life transitions, theoretical perspectives and coaching approaches. Chapters in Part I cover specific life transitions or stages, covering both theoretical and applied perspectives. Each chapter includes a coaching case study, outlining practical examples of 'developmental coaching'. Part II covers themes and topics that transcend particular transitions, namely positive psychology and generations in the workplace.

## Part I: Developmental coaching – transitions and turning points

### Chapter 2: Childhood transitions and celebrating strengths (Jenny Fox Eades)

This chapter outlines the range of transitions faced by children and focuses on experiences of school. Jenny Fox Eades shares an innovative, positive psychology-based programme that coaches the school as an organisation. She draws on anthropology, psychoanalysis and the tradition of story telling. The case study shows this approach in practice and demonstrates the positive impact on childhood resilience.

### Chapter 3: Coaching through the teenage years (Angela Puri)

Angela Puri discusses the pressures and opportunities experienced during teenage transitions. She considers the factors that affect the generation of teenagers growing up today, such as the pervasive influence of social networking. The case study discusses the use of cognitive-behavioural techniques in the context of transition.

### Chapter 4: From twenties to thirties (Sheila Panchal)

Early adulthood is the topic of this chapter. Two transitions are reviewed: the 'early 20s' and the 'turning 30' transitions. Specific challenges pertaining to career, relationships, health and lifestyle are covered. Two case studies are included: one focuses on an individual coachee, and the other examines a group coaching programme in an organisational setting.

### Chapter 5: Becoming a parent (Jennifer Liston-Smith)

Unlike other transition points, becoming a parent is a uniquely optional transition but is one that many experience in their lifetime. Jennifer Liston-Smith reviews theory and research in the area, considering the experience of both mothers and fathers. Her case study highlights the value of coaching in supporting the maternity transition.

## Chapter 6: Modern mid-life (Emma Donaldson-Feilder and Sheila Panchal)

Myths and preconceptions associated with the mid-life crisis are examined and the reality of experience for today's mid-lifers is discussed. The benefits of mindfulness, acceptance and being in the moment as coaching strategies are brought to light in the case study.

## Chapter 7: Looking forward to retirement (Siobhain O'Riordan)

Siobhain O'Riordan considers the multi-dimensional and changing nature of retirement. Our increasing longevity is noted as a significant influence on the nature of this life stage. The range of contexts and settings for retirement and third-age coaching is explored and a practical example is illustrated in the case study.

## Part II: Developmental coaching – themes and applications

### Chapter 8: Positive psychology and strengths coaching through transition (P. Alex Linley, Robert Biswas-Diener and Emma Trenier)

Positive psychology is central to 'developmental coaching' and is a theme running through many of the chapters. This chapter focuses on positive psychology and the specific application of the discipline to coaching through transition. Strengths coaching is a particular focus, illustrated in relation to the transition of redundancy.

### Chapter 9: Managing generations (Ben Green and Helen Williams)

This chapter looks at the co-existence of the four generations in the workplace and strategies to effectively manage a cross-generational workforce. Characteristics and motivators of different generations are reviewed and the implications of these differences for organisations and managers are highlighted.

## Commonalities, differences and linkages

O'Riordan and Panchal (2007) have discussed a number of commonalities, differences and linkages between the 'turning 30' and retirement transition points, which can be broadened to encapsulate all of the transitions. For developmental coaches, it is helpful to consider common points amongst transitions and any key differences and useful linkages that can be made in the coachee's mind with previous or future transitions.

Focusing on strengths has been mentioned across the board, and this is one consistent element across transitions. From a child starting school to a mid-life father adjusting to life without dependent children, all benefit from identifying and applying strengths and transferable skills to move forward. Also, physical changes are typically associated with transitions, from the major changes associated with teenage years or later life, to the more subtle changes that may occur in early adulthood. For women in particular, the impact of the 'biological clock' and fertility can affect adulthood transitions.

Perhaps the most central commonalities across transitions are questions of identity (who am I?) and purpose (why am I?), linking to Erikson's (1950) theory. The need to re-examine the self-concept and set new goals seems important. The notions of expectation and choice are related to this. Individuals may reflect on what is expected of them – at school, starting university, as they approach 30, as a parent, in mid-life, in retirement – and consider the plethora of choices available. In light of these factors, individuals are challenged to make decisions that are congruent with their values, identity and purpose. O'Riordan and Panchal (2007) suggested that lifespan development as a whole could be considered as a 'man's search for meaning' (from Frankl, 1959), with search and re-evaluation of purpose as a key driver throughout.

Differences between transitions exist in the specific challenges and opportunities faced. Young adults are likely to be concerned with establishing a career, whereas decline in health is more likely to be associated with mid-life and retirement. In addition, differential levels of self-knowledge may be accessible to individuals. Transitions and experiences in teenage years are likely to shape and inform an individual about their personality, values, strengths and skills. Later transitions can draw on the wisdom of earlier years and transitions. Kloep and Hendry (2007) suggest that skills demonstrated by those who adjust successfully in retirement are learnt earlier in the lifespan.

Another potential difference relates to accumulation versus letting go of roles. As a child, generally a key role is that of son or daughter. With subsequent childhood, teenage and early adulthood transitions these roles are added to – student, sibling, friend, employee, partner, parent and so on. With middle to late adulthood transitions these roles may reduce. Parental and career responsibility diminishes and an element of 'letting go' is required.

Transitions tend to involve taking stock of the past, considering the present and looking to the future. While this may be a commonality, the extent to which the past, present and future are examined may depend on the life stage. Earlier transitions may focus more on the present, with the future and past increasingly coming into effect. For example, the 'turning 30' transition is often a time when individuals consider their future seriously for the first time. Later transitions may be concerned with the past and present. In retirement, one may reflect back on life's experiences and achievements as well as savouring day-to-day living, if not impaired by significant ill-health. Whilst there are individual differences in time orientation, these broad trends could apply. Zimbardo and Boyd (2008) categorised differences in time orientation. They suggest that the optimum time perspective is high on past-positive, moderately high on future, moderate on present-hedonism and low on past-negative and present-fatalistic. Exploring time orientations during life transitions can be a useful perspective for coaches. Past-negative orientations where people become enmeshed in regrets can make transitional times more challenging.

A related concept is 'death awareness', in that as we age we tend to be more aware of death and its inevitability. While this can cause anxiety, it can also be a catalyst for living more purposefully. Kubler-Ross (1975: 164) believes that it is important for us to face our own mortality in order to live fully:

It is the denial of death that is partially responsible for living empty, purposeless lives; for when you live as if you will live forever, it becomes too easy to postpone the things that you know you must do. You live your life in preparation for tomorrow or remembrance of yesterday, and meanwhile each day is lost. In contrast when you fully understand that each day you awaken could be the last you have, you take the time that day to grow, to become more of who you really are, to reach out to other human beings.

A growing sense that time is limited is common during the 'turning 30' and 'mid-life' transitions, which prompts reflection and a sense of agency, especially if a person has experienced a close bereavement. Perhaps this view goes some way to explain research that has found psychological well-being to be U-shaped across the lifespan, with a dip in middle age (Blanchflower and Oswald, 2008). The optimism associated with seeing life stretch ahead of you in youth and the purposeful living of old age may contrast with more challenging, searching times in middle adulthood.

Finally, some transitions are linked to legislation, for example retirement and work-related maternity. Both retirement and maternity are personal transitions that have a legislative framework and require support from employers that often is not available. Childhood and teenage transitions also rely on institutional support, from schools and colleges.

In line with research by Kloep and Hendry (2006) and the assumptions underlying lifespan development theories, we can assume linkages and continuity between the transitions. Successful negotiation of one transition can set up success for future changes. As such, coaches working with an individual on a particular turning point can have a much broader and lasting impact on their development and life satisfaction. Individuals experiencing any transition can benefit from support, from family, friends and organisations. For many, this support can be lacking, which is where developmental coaches have an increasingly important role.

## Integrated model for developmental coaches

A model to support our view of 'developmental coaching' can be found in Figures 1.1 and 1.2. This integrates insights and learning from key theories and practical approaches, and provides a framework for coaches who are operating as 'developmental coaches'. Figure 1.1 (Transitions Continuum) combines generational factors and life transitions so that a coach can identify where a particular coachee could be placed, and therefore what types of developmental and social

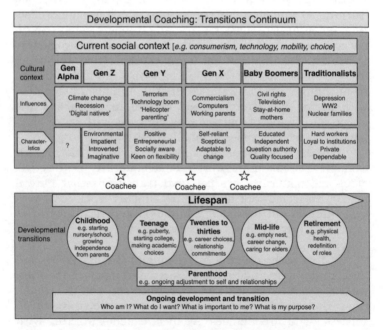

*Figure 1.1* Developmental Coaching: Transitions Continuum

| Developmental Coaching: INSIGHT Framework | | |
| --- | --- | --- |
| **Goal:** To facilitate a positive experience of transition and enable self-management of future transitions | | |
| **Element** | **Aims** | **Example techniques** |
| **I**ncrease self-knowledge | To gain greater self-insight and highlight the value of this as a basis for life decisions (vs external expectations). | Exercises/psychometrics to surface values, strengths, motivators, drivers etc. Lifeline tools to promote learning from past transitions. |
| **N**ormalise transitions | To counter feelings of isolation by creating awareness of life transitions as an integral aspect of development, and acknowledge range of associated emotions. | Discussion of developmental models (e.g. Erikson, 1950) or transition models (e.g. Bridges, 1995). |
| **S**upport positive coping | To build effective coping strategies to deal with challenges of transition. | Strategies could include health (nutrition/exercise), social support, relaxation and cognitive re-assessment. |
| **I**ntegrate past, present, future | To promote positive evaluations of the past, present and future. | Gratitude exercises (past), taking stock/optimism (present) and vision/purpose (future). Discussion of possible selves, time orientations and life stories/links across transitions. |
| **G**ive time and space | To allow sufficient time and space to work through the process of transition. | Mindfulness and acceptance and commitment techniques. Creating opportunities for reflection. |
| **H**ighlight broader context | To draw attention to broader influences and expectations impacting experience of transition. | Review relevant cultural and generational factors. Identify expectations of key individuals/society and surface coachee's own expectations. |
| **T**ailor solutions | To enable sustainable change via goals, strategies and solutions. | Goal setting, solution-focused questioning, action plans, understanding the process of change and celebration of success. |

*\* Not all of these elements will be relevant for all transitions and individuals. Coaches can select the elements that may support their coachee most effectively.*

*Figure 1.2* **Developmental Coaching: INSIGHT Framework**

context may be helpful to understand. Figure 1.2 (INSIGHT Framework) outlines different techniques that can be applied to 'developmental coaching', drawing from coaching and positive psychology.

It is important to note that there is not a 'one size fits all' approach. Not all the concepts will be relevant for any particular transition. Furthermore, as emphasised previously, individual differences must be respected and stereotypical assumptions avoided. However, this framework should offer some useful insights and be considered as a menu or toolkit of resources.

Further theoretical and practical questions merit future consideration and research, to advance our understanding of how to effectively support individuals through key life transitions. Such questions have been raised by O'Riordan and Panchal (2008):

• How much 'big picture' knowledge is useful to us as coaches and coaching psychologists?

- Does the personal experience of a particular life transition point help to coach others? Do I need to have experienced what you have in order to help you?
- How do we avoid age-based stereotypes when coaching?
- As coaches, what impact are we having, if any, on future generations?
- How might life transitions differ across cultures, and what are the implications for coaches?

Some of these questions are reflected on throughout the book. For example, in Chapter 5 Jennifer Liston-Smith describes how the fact that the parent coach is a parent him or herself can help to create empathy, but on the flipside the coach must resist the urge to give advice and make assumptions based on their own experiences. As for all coaching, good supervision is essential to ensure that developmental coaches are aware of, and addressing, these issues.

## Supporting transitions

'Developmental coaching' is one of a number of social support mechanisms that may be employed by individuals during transition. People may draw on support from partners, parents, family and friends or self-help groups. Mentoring by an older, more experienced individual is a strategy advocated by Levinson (1986), notably in early adulthood. He notes that a mentor is ideally half a generation older than the individual, as with a greater age gap they may represent a parenting figure. Cross-generational interaction in family, social and work settings can be a reciprocal process where two people can learn from each other about how to deal with particular issues, problems or transitions. Generational psychology is an area that could inform coaching and mentoring practice. Individuals may also seek therapists when facing particular difficulty in negotiating the questions and challenges associated with transition (e.g. Sugarman, 1986, 2010).

'Developmental coaching' has a role to play alongside these other sources of help, yet coaches need to be mindful of appropriate boundaries with counselling, therapy in particular, and make referrals as appropriate. Again, supervision can help coaches to surface and deal with such issues. A good understanding of the coach–coachee relationship and the ability to apply that theory and knowledge to the practice of developmental coaching can help the coach to support the coachee during times of transition (see Palmer and McDowall, 2010). Similar to other forms of coaching, developmental coaching has a caveat; the coaching conversation should focus on the coachee's issues and goals and, although it is important for the coach's practice to be informed by theory and research, the goals should not be coach driven.

## In conclusion

In this chapter, we have introduced our view of 'developmental coaching' and shared relevant theory and research, majoring on lifespan development and generational perspectives. Book chapters have been reviewed and similarities, differences and linkages between transitions have been explored. Finally, an integrated 'developmental coaching' model has been presented, which can be a useful resource for coaches working within this field. 'Developmental coaching' is a broad and evolving aspect of coaching and coaching psychology that merits further exploration and consideration. As coaches, we have a unique and exciting opportunity to help coachees maximise the developmental potential of the inevitable transitions and turning points they will experience during their lifespan, create positive life stories and enjoy meaningful and fulfilled lives.

## Discussion issues

1  What are the key theories that inform coaching during transitions?
2  Are life transitions inherently stressful?
3  How might a legislative framework have an impact upon transitions in life?
4  In what way is the 'big picture' knowledge useful to coaches and coaching psychologists?

## References

Bachkirova, T. (2010) The cognitive-developmental approach to coaching. In E. Cox, T. Bachkirova and D. Clutterbuck (Eds.), *The Complete Handbook of Coaching* (pp. 132–145). London: Sage.

Bachkirova, T. and Cox, E. (2007) A cognitive-developmental approach for coach development. In S. Palmer and A. Whybrow (Eds.), *Handbook of Coaching Psychology: A Guide for Practitioners* (pp. 325–350). London: Routledge.

Bacon, T. J. (2003) Helping people change. *Industrial and Commercial Training, 35*(2): 73–77.

Blanchflower, D. G. and Oswald, A. J. (2008) Is well-being U-shaped over the life cycle? *Social Science and Medicine, 66*: 1733–1749.

Bridges, W. (1995) *Managing Transitions: Making the Most of Change*. London: Nicholas Brealey Publishing.

CIPD (2008) *Gen Up: How the Four Generations Work*. London: Chartered Institute of Personnel and Development. Retrieved from http://www.cipd.co.uk/onlineinfodocuments on 10 January 2009.

Cox, E. and Jackson, P. (2010) Developmental coaching. In E. Cox, T. Bachkirova and D. Clutterbuck (Eds.), *The Complete Handbook of Coaching* (pp. 217–230). London: Sage.

Erikson, E. (1950) *Childhood and Society*. New York: Norton.

Erikson, E. (1995) *Childhood and Society*. London: Vintage.

Frankl, V. (1959) *Man's Search for Meaning*. London: Random House.

Frankl, V. (1963) *Man's Search for Meaning: An Introduction to Logo Therapy*. New York: Washington Square Press.

Fromm, E. (1976) *To Have or To Be*. London: Continuum Books.

Garvey, B. (2009) Coaching people through life transitions. In J. Passmore (Ed.), *Diversity in Coaching Working with Gender, Culture, Race and Age* (pp. 255–272). London: Kogan Page.

Grant, A. M. and Cavanagh, M. (2004) Toward a profession of coaching: Sixty-five years of progress and challenges for the future. *International Journal of Evidence-Based Coaching and Mentoring, 2*: 7–21.

Hendry, L. B. and Kloep, M. (2002) *Life-Span Development: Resources, Challenges and Risks*. London: Thomson Learning.

Holmes, T. H. and Rahe, R. H. (1967) Social Readjustment Rating Scale. *Journal of Psychosomatic Research, 11*: 213–218.

House of Commons (1999) *A Century of Change: Trends in UK Statistics since 1900*. Retrieved from http://www.parliament.uk/commons/lib/research/rp99/rp99-111.pdf on 3 January 2009.

Jacques, E. (1965) Death and the midlife crisis. *International Journal of Psychoanalysis, 46*: 502–514.

James, W. (2007) *Affluenza*. London: Vermillion.

Jung, C. G. and De Laszlo, V. S. (1958) *Psyche and Symbol: A Selection from the Writings of C.G. Jung*. Garden City, NY: Doubleday.
Jung, C. G. and De Laszlo, V. S. (1959) *Basic Writings*. New York: Modern Library.
Kaplan, B. (1983) A trio of trials. In R. M. Lerner (Ed.), *Developmental Psychology: Historical and Philosophical Perspectives* (pp. 185–239). Hillsdale, NJ: Lawrence Erlbaum Associates, Inc.
Kauffman, C., Boniwell, I. and Silberman, J. (2010) The positive psychology approach to coaching. In E. Cox, T. Bachkirova and D. Clutterbuck (Eds.), *The Complete Handbook of Coaching* (pp. 158–171). London: Sage.
Kegan, R. (1982) *The Evolving Self: Problems and Process in Human Development*. London: Harvard University Press.
Kegan, R. (1994) *In Over our Heads*. London: Harvard University Press.
Kloep, M. and Hendry, L. B. (2006) Entry or exit? Transitions into retirement. *Journal of Occupational and Organizational Psychology, 79*: 569–593.
Kloep, M. and Hendry, L. B. (2007) Retirement a new beginning? *The Psychologist, 20*: 742–745.
Knowles, M. S., Holton, E. F. and Swanson, R. A. (2005) *The Adult Learner: The Definitive Classic in Adult Education and Human Resource Development* (6th ed.). Burlington, MA: Elsevier.
Kubler-Ross, E. (1969) *On Death and Dying*. London: Macmillan.
Kubler-Ross, E. (1975) *Death: The Final Stage of Growth*. Englewood Cliffs, NJ: Prentice-Hall.
Laske, O. (2008) On the unity of behavioural and developmental perspectives in coaching: A view from the constructive developmental framework. *International Coaching Psychology Review, 3*: 125–147.
Leonard-Cross, E. (2010) Developmental coaching: Business benefit – fact or fad? An evaluative study to explore the impact of coaching in the workplace. *International Coaching Psychology Review, 5*: 36–47.
Levinson, D. J. (1986) A conception of adult development. *American Psychologist, 41*: 3–13.
Levy, B. R., Slade, M. D., Kunkel, S. R. and Kasl, S. V. (2002) Longevity increased by positive self-perceptions of aging. *Journal of Personality and Social Psychology, 83*: 261–270.
Linley, P. A. and Harrington, S. (2007) Integrating positive psychology and coaching psychology: Shared assumptions and aspirations? In S. Palmer and A. Whybrow (Eds.), *Handbook of Coaching Psychology: A Guide for Practitioners* (pp. 40–56). London: Routledge.

Loevinger, J. (1976) *Ego Development: Conceptions and Theories*. San Francisco, CA: Jossey-Bass.

Markus, H. and Nurius, P. (1986) Possible selves. *American Psychologist*, *41*: 954–969.

Merriam, S. B. (1998) Adult life transitions: Opportunities for learning and development. In M. A. Wolf and M. A. Leahy (Eds.), *Adults in Transition* (pp. 8–18). Washington, DC: American Association for Adult and Continuing Education.

Office for National Statistics (2009) *Latest of Life Expectancy*. Retrieved from http://www.statistics.gov.uk/CCI/nugget.asp?ID=168 on 18 January 2010.

O'Riordan, S. and Panchal, S. (2007, 17 December) *Managing Milestones: Enabling Coaching Psychologists to Understand Generations and Support Positive Life Transitions – from 'Turning 30' to 'Retirement'*. Paper presented at SGCP 3rd National Coaching Psychology Conference, City University, London.

O'Riordan, S. and Panchal, S. (2008, 17 December) *The Big Picture: Placing Life Transitions in Today's Generational Context for Coaching Psychologists*. Paper presented at SGCP 1st European Coaching Psychology Conference, University of Westminster, London.

Palmer, S. (2006) *Toxic Childhood: How the Modern World is Damaging our Children and What We Can Do About It*. London: Orion.

Palmer, S. and Cooper, C. (2010) *How to Deal with Stress*. London: Kogan Page.

Palmer, S. and Gyllensten, K. (2010) Counselling psychology in the workplace. In R. Woolfe, S. Strawbridge, B. Douglas and W. Dryden (Eds.), *Handbook of Counselling Psychology* (pp. 416–433). London: Sage.

Palmer, S. and McDowall, A. (2010) *The Coaching Relationship: Putting People First*. Hove: Routledge.

Piaget, J. (1972) Intellectual evolution from adolescence to adulthood. *Human Development*, *15*: 1–21.

Reese, H. W. and Overton, W. F. (1970) Models of development and theories of development. In L. R. Goulet and P. B. Baltes (Eds.), *Life-span Developmental Psychology: Research and Theory* (pp. 115–145). New York: Academic Press.

Schlossberg, N. K., Waters, E. B. and Goodman, J. (1995) *Counseling Adults in Transition* (2nd ed.). New York: Springer.

Schwartz, B. (2003) *The Paradox of Choice: Why More is Less*. New York: Ecco.

Schwartz, B., Ward. A, Monterosso, J., Lyubomirsky, S., White, K. and Lehman, D. P. R. (2002) Maximising vs satisficing: Happiness is a matter of choice. *Journal of Personality and Social Psychology*, *83*: 1178–1197.

Seligman, M. (2003) *Authentic Happiness*. London: Nicholas Brealey Publishing.

Seligman, M., Reivich, K., Jaycox, L. and Gillham, J. (1995) *The Optimistic Child: A Proven Program to Safeguard Children Against Depression and Build Lifelong Resilience*. New York: Houghton-Mifflin.

Seligman, M. E. P., Steen, T. A., Park, N. and Peterson, C. (2005) Positive psychology progress: Empirical validation of interventions. *American Psychologist*, *60*: 410–421.

Sheehy, G. (1976) *Passages: Predictable Crises of Adult Life*. New York: Dutton.

Sheehy, G. (1995) *New Passages: Mapping your Life across Time*. London: Random House.

Stanley, N., Mallon, S., Bell, J. and Manthorpe, J. (2009) Trapped in transition: Findings from a UK study of student suicide. *British Journal of Guidance and Counselling*, *37*: 419–433.

Strenger, S. and Ruttenberg, A. (2008) The existential necessity of mid-life change. *Harvard Business Review*, *86*: 82–90.

Sugarman, L. (1986) *Lifespan Development: Frameworks, Accounts and Strategies*. London: Methuen.

Sugarman, L. (1996) Narratives of theory and practice: The psychology of life-span development. In R. Woolfe and W. Dryden (Eds.), *Handbook of Counselling Psychology* (pp. 287–306). London: Sage.

Sugarman, L. (2001) *Life-Span Development: Frameworks, Accounts and Strategies*. Hove: Psychology Press.

Sugarman, L. (2010) The life course: A framework for the practice of counselling psychology. In R. Woolfe, S. Strawbridge, B. Douglas and W. Dryden (Eds.), *Handbook of Counselling Psychology* (pp. 279–297). London: Sage.

Sugarman, L. and Wolfe, R. (1989) Piloting the stream: The life cycle and counselling. In S. Palmer and G. McMahon (Eds.), *Handbook of Counselling* (pp. 22–36). Hove: Tavistock/Routledge.

Thomas, R. M. (1990) *Counseling and Life-Span Development*. Newbury Park, CA: Sage.

Wikipedia (2010) *Generation Z*. Retrieved from http://en.wikipedia. org/wiki/Generation_Z on 7 January 2010.

Zimbardo, P. and Boyd, J. (2008) *The Time Paradox: The New Psychology of Time that will Change your Life*. New York: Free Press.

## Recommended reading

Bachkirova, T. (2010) The cognitive-developmental approach to coaching. In E. Cox, T. Bachkirova and D. Clutterbuck (Eds.), *The Complete Handbook of Coaching* (pp. 132–145). London: Sage.

Bachkirova, T. and Cox, E. (2007) A cognitive-developmental approach for coach development. In S. Palmer and A. Whybrow (Eds.), *Handbook of Coaching Psychology: A Guide for Practitioners* (pp. 325–350). London: Routledge.

Cox, E. and Jackson, P. (2010) Developmental coaching. In E. Cox, T. Bachkirova and D. Clutterbuck (Eds.), *The Complete Handbook of Coaching* (pp. 217–230). London: Sage.

Garvey, B. (2009) Coaching people through life transitions. In J. Passmore (Ed.), *Diversity in Coaching: Working with Gender, Culture, Race and Age* (pp. 255–272). London: Kogan Page.

Kauffman, C., Boniwell, I. and Silberman, J. (2010) The positive psychology approach to coaching. In E. Cox, T. Bachkirova and D. Clutterbuck (Eds.), *The Complete Handbook of Coaching* (pp. 158–171). London: Sage.

Kubler-Ross, E. (1969) *On Death and Dying.* London: Macmillan.

Linley, P. A. and Harrington, S. (2010) Integrating positive psychology and coaching psychology: Shared assumptions and aspirations? In S. Palmer and A. Whybrow (Eds.), *Handbook of Coaching Psychology: A Guide for Practitioners* (pp. 40–56). London: Routledge.

Strenger, S and Ruttenberg, A. (2008) The existential necessity of mid-life change. *Harvard Business Review, 86*: 82–90.

Sugarman, L. (2001) *Life-Span Development: Frameworks, Accounts and Strategies.* Hove: Psychology Press.

Sugarman, L. (2010) The life course: A framework for the practice of counselling psychology. In R. Woolfe, S. Strawbridge, B. Douglas and W. Dryden (Eds.), *Handbook of Counselling Psychology* (pp. 279–297). London: Sage.

# Part I

# Developmental coaching – transitions and turning points

# Childhood transitions and celebrating strengths

*Jenny Fox Eades*

## A model for a coach working with a primary school

A child's coaches are its parents or principal caregivers and then its teachers. These are the adults who will help a child develop and realise their potential. This chapter will look at how a third adult, a 'school strengths coach', can work with primary schools to coach children *indirectly*, through working with the institution (i.e. the school) to which they belong. The approach used (now called Celebrating Strengths) did not start life as a coaching programme, but as a series of workshops designed to promote children's positive mental health. The programme evolved by drawing on various theoretical traditions while underpinned by a practical emphasis on what 'worked' in the classroom and the school. This chapter will describe these theoretical traditions, explore the evolutionary process of the programme and draw conclusions about the value of making 'school strengths coaches' available more widely to schools.

## Childhood as a time of constant transition

Childhood is a time of transition and schools are organisations in transition. They are changing constantly and at a faster rate than at any other time in their lifespan. They are changing physically and emotionally. Their capacity to communicate is still developing. They are learning about themselves and their limits, about other people and how to live alongside them and about the tools that our society considers necessary for adult life (Wilson, 2003).

At home, children encounter many transitions. The birth of new siblings means that children must adjust to a different position and role within their family. Parents may begin or cease employment, producing change in the family dynamic that children sense but may not understand. Break-up or divorce can result in a new home or different living arrangements and a principal care-giver who is undergoing a major transition of their own (Allatt, 1996).

And then the child starts nursery or school for the first time and has to negotiate becoming part of a large organisation. Each year may bring a new teacher and new class group to work with.

Starting school can be a particularly challenging time for children, particularly if it coincides, as it often does, with other major transitions. One young boy the author worked with in his first year of school is a good example of how stressful this time of life can be for children. In starting school he was joining an organisation of 400 individuals when his previous largest community had been a playgroup of 20. His mother had just had a new baby so his life was changing from 'only child' to 'oldest child' in the family – with different amounts of attention and different expectations. His father was working away Monday to Friday, and because 4-year-olds have very little concept of time he was unsure when, exactly, he would see his father again. The family were planning to move house to follow the father's job. The boy, a bright, usually confident, very well loved child, became unhappy and with-drawn. Adults do not like to consider children as suffering from 'stress' but he was. The large school assemblies became overwhelming for him. We managed that situation by intro-ducing a small 'ritual' – the head teacher spoke to him indi-vidually as soon as he sat down and gave him her papers to hold – that made him feel known and safe. On the author's suggestion the parents made a simple calendar with a sheet for each day, Monday to Friday, so that he could physically tear each one off and see when daddy would be home. This also helped him feel more secure.

The vast majority of children cope admirably with the stress of starting school – it is scary but it is more *exciting* than scary and most children are very resilient. But the stress is real and if other factors combine to increase that stress then children, like the boy above, can react badly. The decrease in family stability in recent years means that more children than before are facing transitions such as starting school against a backdrop of other transitions such as moving house, a parent moving out or a change in siblings (Simpson, 1994). Most children will still cope admirably but there is scope for ensuring that schools understand how to support them best.

## School as a place of transition

The school of which that child is part is also in transition. Each year a large number of new children join a school while others leave. Each new member and each departure subtly changes the tone and composition of the organisation as a whole. Adults swap roles, new staff join, children change year group and see themselves and are seen by adults differently. Children in the final year begin mentally and emotionally to prepare themselves for their major transition to high school or junior school from September onwards. *For a school, stability is unusual and change is the norm.*

Children also negotiate 'minor' transitions on a daily basis: the transition from home to school and back again each day; the transition from the comfort of the classroom to the large and possibly frightening space that is the playground; the transition from the structure of term time to holiday and back again.

A coach working with a primary school is working with a community facing almost constant transition. A framework for thinking about and working with these transitions was developed by combining insights from a variety of theoretical traditions with some ancient human practices. The theoretical traditions are psychodynamic theory, positive psychology and anthropology; the ancient practices are those of oral story telling and community celebration or 'celebrations'.

## Learning as a kind of transition

Learning is a mixed experience, a complex blend of anxiety and excitement, and hope and passion. For learning to take place we need to be able to cope with uncertainty, the pain of not understanding and the risk of potential failure. At the same time the teacher's love and passion for the subject offer an incentive to keep going through the boring, difficult or anxious parts. There is excitement in learning something new, the thrill of mastery, the hope that I will succeed. Learning may be thought about as a transition in its own right – the move from 'not understanding' to 'understanding' – and it is undertaken daily in schools up and down the country with all the attendant anxiety that transitions always bring.

## Psychodynamic thinking and the emotional life of a primary school

Psychodynamic theory provided the starting point for thinking about anxiety in primary schools and about the different levels of school life – the individual level, the class group and the school as a whole.

A psychodynamic perspective considers the effect of early experiences and the unconscious on behaviour and emotion (Salzberger-Wittenberg, Williams and Osborne, 1983). Transitions produce a mixture of emotions: a combination of sadness for the stage that is passing, anxiety about what the next stage will bring and hope for future possibilities. Previous transitions – experiences of loss and new beginnings – affect adults and children alike when they encounter new transitions in the present. Earlier emotions return and amplify present ones. These unconscious echoes help to explain the powerful emotions that often attend transitions – feelings of helplessness, of getting lost, of not being liked or understood, of being inadequate for the task ahead. At the same time each new beginning carries the potential for growth and for positive outcomes – it is exciting and full of possibility.

Even little transitions (e.g. the start or end of a day) can bring with them echoes of the emotions that attend major transitions, and for children for whom transitions have been problematic in the past these occasions can cause heightened anxiety. Adults working with children can experience a lot of anxiety on a daily basis that they sense and pick up from their pupils. It is distinct from their own anxiety – it is 'transferred' anxiety – but it may amplify pre-existing anxieties of their own.

'Transference' is the term used to describe how we transfer feelings from past experiences into the present. Children 'transfer' some of the feelings they have for their parents onto their teachers, and some of the feelings they have for their siblings onto their classmates. Transference can be positive, for example when relationships and feelings in the past have been predominantly positive, or it can be negative, such as when relationships and early emotions were less benign.

As adults we also experience transference when people we meet and work with remind us in subtle ways of other people from our past and evoke 'transferred' emotions – feelings not really caused by the person in front of us but by someone from long ago. The groups we are part of remind us of earlier groups, our family group in particular, and those early group experiences can be 'transferred' into the present.

A school consists of many inter-related groups, each with its own emotional mix, and is also part of other groups, one of which is society as a whole. Part of the role of a school coach is to think about how these groups influence one another and work together. One consideration needs to be how the very mixed feelings about education, teachers and children in our society affect the life of the school.

## Education today

There is confusion about the purpose of education in our society and ambiguity in how we think of children. Is education a good thing in itself, a remedy for poor parenting or a way of giving skills to the workforce of the future? Are children little angels to cosset and protect from crossing roads or 'feral' creatures that we need protecting from? Society sends schools mixed messages about their purpose and their members and this is a cause of anxiety.

In the past 20 years government initiatives have raised anxiety further. There have been strategies, targets, league tables and a focus on delivering curriculum content rather than on the creative process of the teacher – an emphasis on highly structured lessons rather than following pupil interest. This has made it harder for teachers to use their initiative and creativity or to think about and respond to the needs of each child (Boyle and Charles, 2008).

More recently, various government initiatives have tried to address this lack of creativity and individual focus on the child. In 2008 Boyle and Charles surveyed 4000 primary schools to see what changes this had made to teaching practice and found little evidence of any change at all:

> Teachers have strategies . . . and they have frameworks to plan to and from and they have centrally supplied schemes of work to save the 'tedium' of matching teaching material to developmental or interest levels, in short they have been reduced to technicians. Above all, they are quick to tell us, if they follow these formulae they are 'safe and secure' in their accountability and auditing processes conducted by their own Senior Leadership Team. So, in summary, the central purpose for becoming a teacher has been lost.

Institutions (like individuals) deal with anxiety by forming defences against it. Paradoxically, government initiatives have both *increased* teacher anxiety and also *produced a defensive mechanism* for dealing with it. If teachers follow rigid schemes of work they feel safe and protect themselves from the anxiety of failing. What also happens, regrettably, is that they do not enjoy their work as much because it is less creative. They have less rewarding relationships with students because there is not the time to get to know them that there used to be and 'enjoying each other's company and getting to know each other' is not a target and is not included in any scheme of work. Teachers no longer have the freedom to follow their own deep enthusiasms in the classroom so they find it harder to inspire children with a deep love of learning – for how inspiring can a centrally planned worksheet ever be?

## Anxiety and hope

The challenge for the coach in a primary school is to work with the institution to contain some of the anxiety that is being felt by teachers and pupils alike so that there is more space for reflection and playful experimentation – more space for the hopeful, passionate and creative aspects of learning to come through. If children feel too much anxiety then they cannot afford to be interested, passionate or to experiment or challenge themselves. This fear of failure makes it hard for them to experience or develop a love for genuine learning.

Too much anxiety on the part of the teacher means that they play it safe, sticking to the scheme or the worksheet. In order to achieve real excellence, to help children genuinely move from 'not knowing' to 'knowing', teachers too must feel safe enough to fail sometimes and risk the occasional moment of chaos. The coach helps to create an environment in which teachers feel safe enough to move away from 'following a formula of planned predictability . . . delivered to passive children' (Boyle and Charles, 2008) and to engage in the messy, complex and exciting business that is education.

In order to work with a school the coach needs an approach that can contain anxiety and support hope, that can work at the many levels of the school simultaneously while accommodating the different levels of the child's experience – working alone, working in small groups, working as a class and feeling part of a whole school. In effect the coach needs ways of working that allow him or her to coach 'the school' as well as the individuals within it.

## Oral story telling as a coaching tool

Oral story telling and traditional tales provide one way of working at different levels of the child's experience while containing anxiety and promoting hope throughout the school. In *The Uses of Enchantment*, Bettelheim (1976), a psychologist working with children, explored the importance of fairy tales for children's psychological development and described how a story could itself become a 'container' – somewhere to put our fears and the parts of ourselves, such as hate and aggression, that we feel uncomfortable with. At the same time, classic fairy tales are profoundly hopeful, providing examples of ordinary characters who overcome obstacles and survive adversity. *Story telling can be seen as the oldest coaching intervention known to humanity.*

Story telling is a perfect tool to introduce into primary schools. Teachers have always told stories. It is an 'educational' thing to do and meets many of the curriculum 'objectives and targets' that teachers are so concerned about. At the same time, stories provide space for thinking about anxiety and hope and what life is all about, and they give adults and children space to reflect and space to play. Story telling is fundamentally playful, playing with words, with props and with character and setting. It is an opportunity for teacher and pupil to enjoy their creativity together.

Story telling works at different levels of a child's experience. It is something they can do individually, in play or in writing. Listening to a teacher tell a story is a nurturing class activity. It is also a whole school experience. Assembly time provides the perfect opportunity for the whole community to gather together to hear and tell stories (traditional or anecdotal) and to enjoy a moment of shared reflection.

Stories also provide a perfect way of *priming* the environment of the school with rich, complex and hopeful metaphors. A study by Bargh, Chen and Burrows (1996) found that the physical environment – the things we see and hear around us – has a direct affect on our behaviour. Students who completed a word puzzle containing words associated with old age, such as wrinkle and zimmer frame, actually slowed down in their movements after completing the puzzle. Students who completed a word puzzle containing words associated with rudeness were quicker to interrupt a researcher than a control group working with neutral words. What these studies emphasise is the importance of what students see and hear around them. Stories prime the environment with hopeful messages.

Oral story telling also embeds psychodynamic principles without needing them to be explicitly taught or thought about by the teacher. The silence in stories (and story telling is as much about silence as it is about words) allows the unconscious to work with the story and to make the characters and actions its own. Children can 'transfer' their feelings about people onto the story characters. They can find space in the story for the angry, fearful or envious parts of themselves that they are not very comfortable with. Transferring these strong emotions into the story provides relief and a way to think about them indirectly. The result is a reduction of anxiety and an increase in the enjoyment of learning.

## Anthropology and community celebrations

All societies have rituals and celebrations that mark transitions and create a feeling of shared community. *Purity and Danger*, by anthropologist Mary Douglas (1966), describes the feelings of discomfort and even fear that are caused by ambivalence – by a thing or a person who crosses boundaries, who is 'neither one thing nor the other'. Human beings love tidy categories – is it animal, vegetable or mineral? We like clear classifications and tidy lists. So any transition can be disturbing, or even dangerous, because it involves crossing boundaries: being 'neither one thing nor the other'.

Communities evolve rituals and celebrations to make transitions clearer, to draw clear lines around 'before and after'. These rituals and traditions fulfil many functions, two of which are the containment of anxiety and the celebration of hope. There are major celebrations around important transitions, such as the transition from one year to the next or for individuals moving from puberty to adulthood. There are also little rituals to mark the passing of the hours: morning and evening, work and the return home.

This insight from anthropology explains why, in addition to introducing oral story telling to a primary school, elaborating and building on its existing rituals and traditions (for individuals, classes and the whole school) provides another practical way of working with anxiety and hope.

Schools already have traditions that can be built on and emphasised. New 'traditions' can be invented and introduced. Regular community celebrations give adults and children alike something to look forward to, events apart from the rigidity of the curriculum that still serve educational goals: a way of laying down positive shared memories, containing anxiety and celebrating hope.

Community celebrations traditionally contain story telling, so celebrations complement and enhance the work on stories. From the teacher's perspective, curriculum goals are also being met and the experiences of creating and holding a celebration can feed into and enhance classroom work.

Community celebrations help to mark the major transitions of the school year: from one year to the next, from term to term. Little rituals or celebrations can also help with the minor transitions that children face constantly: 'when we come in from the playground we always sit on the carpet and have a drink of milk'; 'before we go home, Mrs Eades always tells us a story'. Understanding the power of these little celebrations to help make 'minor transitions' a positive experience is an important part of coaching the primary school.

## Positive psychology and strengths-based working

One of the theoretical perspectives that contributed to the development of the work of the school strengths coach and the Celebrating Strengths programme was the area of psychology known as 'positive psychology', specifically the work on strengths by psychologists such as Peterson and Seligman (2004) and Linley and Govindji (2008).

Introducing the formal concept of strengths-based working and the language of strengths into a school is another way of working at all levels of the organisation – we can think about individual strengths, 'our class's strengths' and the strengths of the school. It is another way of priming the environment to have a positive and uplifting effect on the adults and children within that school. Positive psychology, unlike the more abstract concepts of psychodynamic theory, is practical, immediate, tangible and evidence based. It gives teachers straightforward ideas to latch onto and use. It can also, very importantly, help them to meet curriculum goals and targets – those ever-present sources of anxiety to teachers today.

The work on strengths has resonated with both teachers and children – it is simple, positive and uplifting. Good teachers are naturally strengths based, unless so overloaded by anxiety that they have become fixed in defensive and negative thinking. Therefore introducing the concept of a regular focus on strengths builds on what teachers do best.

A strengths approach complements oral story telling because traditional tales are full of larger than life characters who abound in very obvious strengths – and weaknesses! The stories reinforce strengths and provide positive priming, while at the same time the wonderfully flawed characters comfort and contain the listener's anxieties. They make space for our weaknesses to be thought about, even smiled about, as well as our strengths.

Like oral story telling and community celebrations, a focus on strengths helps to manage anxiety and promote a hopeful stance during the almost constant changes and transitions of childhood and school life. A strengths approach is particularly helpful in promoting a positive attitude to learning – whatever the challenge of this particular subject or task, if we know we have strengths and know what they are then our confidence in our ability to succeed and our willingness to persevere is enhanced. A focus on strengths is thus a key element in coaching a school and promoting genuine learning.

## The history of 'Celebrating Strengths'

Celebrating Strengths began in one infant school as a training initiative for staff on the importance of story telling for children's well-being. It developed into classroom visits that staff observed and then spread to three more schools – one infant and two junior.

Once the work on story telling was established, the concept of community celebrations was introduced, followed by the use of a strengths approach based on the Values in Action (VIA) strengths described by Peterson and Seligman (2004). What emerged was a cycle of celebrations, designed in collaboration with the first school, each with some stories and strengths linked to them so that schools could focus on all the strengths in the course of a year.

In a typical visit the coach would hold a whole school assembly, consisting of a story, a focus on one or more strengths and a meditation or reflection based on the strength. Then the coach would visit up to four classrooms in the day, telling stories and using activities incorporating insights from positive psychology. These activities came to be called Strengths Builders, and the combination of stories and Strengths Builders together is now known as Strengths Gym. Teachers were given written materials to support the work but were encouraged to experiment for themselves and to adapt and be creative, not to try to reproduce exactly what the materials suggested or what the coach did.

While the schools' experiences of the early programme were overwhelmingly positive, and an evaluation by Linley and Govindji (2008) demonstrated the benefits of the work, the drawbacks of this approach were also apparent. There was too much emphasis on the coach 'doing' the story telling and strengths work and not enough on transfer of skills. Staff would wait for the coach to visit rather than engage in strengths and story work for themselves. At times some teachers would leave the classroom or sit at the back of the classroom marking work, leaving the coach to act as 'baby sitter'. The focus of the coach at first was on direct work in the classroom with children. Such work, although valued by children and staff, came to be seen by the author as less effective than a focus on the staff and the institution of the school.

It was clear that more space away from the classroom was necessary for staff to understand the different approaches and to explore a strengths perspective for themselves. There was also a need for training so that staff's understanding of the programme increased and they felt confident enough to lead assemblies and to use story telling and Strengths Builders for themselves.

In subsequent schools, this was achieved through a combination of dedicated staff training days, or 'master classes', in the different aspects of the programme and in time set aside for one-to-one work on the teacher's own strengths using the Individual Strengths Assessment developed by the Centre for Applied Positive Psychology (CAPP). This was sometimes followed up by strengths coaching by telephone. Fewer visits by the coach increased the focus on efficient transfer of skills – as well as having the additional benefit to the schools of keeping down the cost of the programme.

## The coach's reflective process

The three theoretical strands of the programme – psychodynamic theory, positive psychology and anthropology and the ancient practical tool of story telling – all contributed to the coach's own reflective processes. Individuals tend to engage in more unconscious and defensive behaviour when under stress, and this is also true of institutions. When schools were experiencing more stressful periods this would be communicated powerfully to the coach through non-verbal means – timetables might be mixed up, communications lost, teachers might 'have to leave' classrooms. The coach would be left feeling confused, inadequate and unvalued, or just overworked. A psychodynamic perspective allowed the coach to see that this was exactly what the teachers were feeling at the time – it was in effect a form of communication. The coach, an outsider, could safely be 'given' these feelings to take away and think about. That she continued to survive these feelings and to come back, positive and enthusiastic, will have contributed to the diminution of anxiety within the institution and its gradual growth towards better functioning.

A focus on the strengths of the children, staff and schools was also an important way of thinking about the work. The tendency to focus on the negative is universal and occurs very strongly when under stress. Working with schools – which are under a lot of stress all the time from both internal and external causes – can generate negativity in the coach. A focus on 'what went well' (one of the Strengths Builders used with teachers and students) by the coach herself allowed a hopeful perspective to be maintained by the coach and communicated to the school.

Anthropologists observe the use of celebrations in different societies to provide markers in the year, to diminish anxiety, to give a focus for the celebration of hope and to internalise values and beliefs. Working in different schools at different stages of the early programme was at times quite disjointed for the coach, who might need to move between very different pieces of work in quick succession. As the programme 'settled down' into a rhythm of celebrations, strengths and stories, the coach could work within a coherent structure of events, facilitating the same celebration and using the same stories at a particular time of year. This not only freed up her thinking space for the personalities and individual challenges of each school, but in itself also proved a satisfying and energising way of working. A focus on cele-bration and seasonality began to develop, not just within the programme but in the coach's own life. She internalised the work on strengths, stories and celebrations herself – exactly the process that the programme is designed to achieve with children and staff in primary schools and with the school itself.

## The story of the schools

As the work progressed it became clear that the stories the schools were telling about themselves were subtly changing. The coach still heard about the stresses and anxieties, but there was also the story of their strengths, their celebrations and the enjoyment of day-to-day work in the classroom. It was a story of growing confidence and enjoyment of school life.

What was also apparent was that each school that used the programme individualised it to suit their own strengths. In one school the celebration programme was of great importance – the celebrations were superbly planned and orchestrated and the strengths were incorporated fully into daily conversations with children. The story work was there but it was less apparent. In another school it was story telling that captured the imagination of staff, that gave additional enjoyment and creativity to each day and that contained anxiety and supported hope for individual staff to the extent that one teacher could say: 'I look forward to coming to school now.'

The coach, an outsider, was using tools that could make space for the different people in the school to think creatively and positively and to engage in learning hopefully. The children were supported by the stories themselves, by the regular, silence-filled assemblies (described as 'cool' by one Year 6 pupil!), by the celebrations and by the focus on their strengths. They were also supported by the renewed enthusiasm and vigour of their staff. Staff were given time to 'play' and to be creative in a way that also met the ubiquitous 'curriculum requirements'. Assemblies were geared as much to *their* need for silence and stillness as to the children's, and the various celebrations were enjoyed by staff as much as by children. One-to-one coaching and an outsider to talk to (a positive, non-judgmental, strengths-focused outsider) served to build hope and confidence.

## Coaching the head teacher

The head teachers of primary schools can feel very isolated. Having another professional to talk to as an equal (an independent professional not employed by the local education authority) provided school leaders with their own opportunity to find the space to think and to be positive. In some cases the programme increased the head's enjoyment of school to the point where they felt restored in their sense of vocation. Making space for the senior leaders of the school to think about their own strengths and the strengths of their school has now been given more prominence within the programme.

### *Case study: Frodingham Infants School*

Frodingham Infants is a state school in Scunthorpe town centre. A high proportion of the children are socially disadvantaged, with poor speech and social skills. Some display highly challenging behaviour.

The head teacher wanted something more for her school and her children – a coherent and positive approach to the whole of school life and a way of enhancing a sense of meaning and spirituality for the school community. At the start of the programme, Year 1 (aged 5–6 years) was seen to be a particularly challenging cohort and there was concern about their academic outcomes. The head teacher heard about Celebrating Strengths from another school and invited us to work with her.

The Celebrating Strengths programme was coming to the end of its pilot phase and it was important to establish whether the observed benefits came purely from the involvement of the coach who devised it or from the programme itself, with its combination of celebrations, strengths and story telling that she had introduced.

Another experienced teacher, with a background in psychology, trained in the approach and began to work in Frodingham, with support and supervision provided by the programme's originator. An introductory Master Class was delivered by the two coaches working together and then the second coach visited the school for 2 days each half term. Coaching days were at first entirely given over to classroom work, but then one-to-one work with staff was introduced and this was increased as the programme developed.

The coach provided email and telephone support for staff in planning community celebrations and the application of strengths-based approaches in the classroom. The school was supplied with teaching materials and stories for each half term, consisting of some theory together with practical ideas for classroom work, assemblies and individual work with children.

### Results of the coaching programme

Frodingham has made extraordinary use of the creative space provided by the visits of the coach and by the introduction of story telling, a strengths perspective and regular celebrations. The school environment is filled with artwork that weaves the stories and strengths together. Teachers research and tell their own stories in addition to those provided by the coach. Staff meetings are conducted from a strengths perspective and strengths are integrated into the whole life and work of the school. Little celebrations, such as focusing on 'What Went Well?' at the end of every day, form part of daily life. The more formal celebrations are a highlight of each term. The transition to junior school is being supported by a focus on strengths. The new teacher is going to visit them at the end of term and the children will start making 'My Top Strengths' posters with her. These will be taken to the new school on the 'transition day visit', completed there and then put up on the wall ready for September.

The children also take home their 'Magic Memory Pearls' at the end of each year. These are simple glass beads made 'special' by the tradition of holding them while thinking of happy memories. One parent reported how her daughter took out her pearl every night for the first 3 weeks she was at junior school and talked to it. It lived by her bed. At the end of that time she began to use it less as she became more secure in her new school.

During the third year of the programme the school had an Ofsted inspection. It moved from 'good with outstanding features' in its previous inspection to 'outstanding'. A key feature of the report was the focus on strengths: 'The cele-bration of strengths extends to staff as well (as pupils) and has been embraced by them so that it is at the core of all the school does.'

The programme has increased teacher and student enjoyment of school, teacher morale and pupil self-esteem. It supports the attainment of academic excellence because it decreases poor behaviour by children and hence the time teachers spend dealing with that behaviour. The 'challenging cohort' of Year 1 students shocked their teachers by getting much better results at the end of Key Stage 2 than had been anticipated. Teachers are explicitly encouraged to use more of their own strengths and to do more of what they love, because it is harder to effectively teach what we do not love.

The head teacher feels that the programme has lowered stress, boosted resilience and increased well-being throughout the school community: 'We celebrate strengths because it makes us feel good inside' (John, aged 6 years). It is a totally voluntary programme, embraced enthusiastically on its own merits and funded by the school with help from the local education authority: 'Celebrating Strengths helps me understand and show my strengths every day and every school should do it' (Molly, aged 5 years).

A focus on little traditions and on strengths has enabled children to 'tell a different story' about themselves. One boy, David, found the transition from home to school each day challenging. He showed high levels of anger and aggression, often at the start of the day or at break times. His head teacher worked with him on his strengths, using stories and a focus on the strength of self-control. She taught him to use the British Sign Language sign for self-control if he found himself getting angry, to 'pull on his reins of self-control'. During the Ofsted inspection, David was pushed by another child but instead of his former behaviour, which would have involved hitting back, he looked around for an adult and ran up to the nearest one available (the inspector). The inspector asked David what he was going to do. David replied: 'I know what to do, I've got to stop, think and pull on my reins of self-control.' The simple use of a little tradition and a focus on a strength has given a 6-year-old boy the ability to reflect positively about himself and to manage the transitions he finds challenging.

## Possible extensions for this approach

The model of coaching described in this chapter evolved in collaboration with primary schools. However, story telling, strengths and celebrations are not just for young children, they are universal. The author is now involved in a project with a high school and a local university, to expand the model to secondary schools. It is possible that similar approaches could be used to help other organisations that experience high levels of stress. Prisons, children's homes and other residential settings could potentially benefit from a coach to help them manage anxiety and promote a strengths-based culture.

Coaching an organisation rather than an individual has meant taking a long- rather than short-term approach to change. After 5 years of running the programme it can be said that the changes that have been introduced are proving durable as well as positive. Traditions can be started, as Celebrating Strengths has shown, and once started they tend to last. Thus, by making sure the traditions we introduce into organisations are positive, we can have an effect that outlasts our involvement and contributes to long-term flourishing. The traditions and approaches that we help to introduce will enable individuals to manage transitions positively well into the future.

## Discussion issues

1  What traditions might a coach introduce or develop in a business setting?
2  Is it possible to coach an individual without considering the groups they belong to?
3  Does an organisation have 'strengths' of its own?
4  Should every school have a 'strengths coach'?

## References

Allatt, P. (1996) Conceptualizing parenting from the standpoint of children: Relationship and transition in the life course. In J. Brannen and M. O'Brian (Eds.), *Children in Families* (pp. 130–144). London: Routledge.

Bargh, J. A., Chen, M. and Burrows, L. (1996) Automaticity of social behaviour: Direct effects of trait construct and stereotype priming on action. *Journal of Personality and Social Psychology*, 71: 230–244.

Bettelheim, B. (1976) *The Uses of Enchantment*. London: Penguin Books.

Boyle, B. and Charles, M. (2008) *Excellence and Enjoyment 2003–2008: A Five Year Review of its Assessment for Learning Strategy: Has it Developed Formative Teaching and Learning in Primary Classrooms?* Manchester: CFAS School of Education, University of Manchester. Available from william.f.boyle@manchester.ac.uk

Douglas, M. (1966) *Purity and Danger: An Analysis of the Concepts of Pollution and Taboo*. London: Routledge.

Linley, P. A. and Govindji, R. (2008) *Average to A+ – Realising Strengths in Yourself and Others*. Coventry: CAPP Press.

Peterson, C. and Seligman, M. E. P. (2004) *Character Strengths and Virtues*. Oxford: Oxford University Press.

Salzberger-Wittenberg, I., Williams, G. and Osborne, E. (1983). *The Emotional Experience of Learning and Teaching*. London: Karnac.

Simpson, B. (1994) Bringing the 'unclear' family into focus: Divorce and re-marriage in contemporary Britain. *Man, 29*: 831–851.

Wilson, P. (2003) *Young Minds in Our Schools*. London: Young Minds.

## Recommended reading

Bettelheim, B. (1976) *The Uses of Enchantment*. London: Penguin Books.

Coren, A. (1997) *A Psychodynamic Approach to Education*. London: Sheldon Press.

Fox Eades, J. M. (2008) *Celebrating Strengths: Building Strengths-Based Schools*. Coventry: CAPP Press.

Linley, P. A. and Govindji, R. (2008) *Average to A+ – Realising Strengths in Yourself and Others*. Coventry: CAPP Press.

Long, R. (2004) *Understanding Child Behaviour*. Salisbury: Quay Books.

Menzies-Lyth, I. (1988) *Containing Anxiety in Institutions: Selected Essays*. London: Free Association Books.

Obholzer, A. and Zagier Roberts, V. (1994) *The Unconscious at Work: Individual and Organisational Stress in the Human Services*. London: Routledge.

Salzberger-Wittenberg, I., Williams, G. and Osborne, E. (1983) *The Emotional Experience of Learning and Teaching*. London: Karnac.

Shapiro, L. and Sprague, R. K. (2009) *The Relaxation and Stress Reduction Workbook for Kids: Help for Children to Cope with Stress, Anxiety, and Transitions*. Oakland, CA: New Harbinger Publications.

# 3

# Coaching through the teenage years

## *Angela Puri*

Mention the teenage years and it is likely that you will evoke some sort of reaction. Whether it is reminiscing about one's own teenage years or a more generic discussion of the 'youth of today', one thing is for certain – teenage years tend to be memorable. Depending on your point of view, these years are either looked upon as the best time of one's life, combining childhood freedom with adult physical maturity, or endured as years of hazard, combining childish behaviour with adult urges!

Interestingly, teenagers have not always been around. The terminology was coined in the first part of the twentieth century and before this people fell into two stages – children and adults. So, although childhood might have had some tender moments, the goal of a child was to grow up as promptly as possible in order to shoulder the responsibilities of an adult.

Teenage years have been used to describe the transitional stage of physical and mental development that occurs between being a child and an adult (Christie and Viner, 2005). However, in recent years the onset of puberty has somewhat increased to pre-adolescence (particularly with females) as well as an occasional extension beyond teenage years (typically with males). This has made the 'teenager' less simple to discern.

Furthermore, the end of adolescence and the beginning of adulthood is relatively unclear (Arnett, 2000). There are different ages at which an individual is considered mature enough to be entrusted with particular tasks (e.g. having sexual relations, voting or marrying) and this may vary by country or culture. So, although the simplistic definition of a teenager covers all those between the ages of 13 and 19 years, for the purpose of this chapter it is defined as the duration of adolescence (the average onset is 12–14 years in girls and 13–15 in boys and, as mentioned earlier, the end of adolescence depends on cultural and individual differences). Generational analysis categorises today's teenagers as Generation Z (see Chapter 1).

## Becoming a teenager

The physical changes that signal the start of adolescence occur alongside psychological and social changes that highlight this stage as being critical in becoming an adult. For example, Freud (1905/1977) focused on psychosexual development, seeing adolescence as a recapitulation of the development of sexual awareness in infancy (Christie and Viner, 2005). Piaget (1972) concentrated largely on cognitive development, seeing the development of abstract thinking abilities as making the transition to independent adult functioning possible. It is during the 'Formal Operational Stage' (11 years onwards) that Piaget believed adolescents begin to move beyond concrete experiences and to think more abstractly, reason logically, draw conclusions from information available as well as working with hypothetical situations. It is believed that the young adult begins to understand things such as love, logical proofs and values. It is also at this stage that the teenager starts to entertain possibilities for the future and is fascinated with who they are and what others think of them (Santrock, 2008).

Erikson (1950) also worked with a life stage model, identifying the tensions around the development of personal identity as central to the notion of adolescence. He highlighted that during adolescence the self-concept goes through dramatic and extensive change and it is during these times that balance is much more difficult to maintain. Erikson (1950) believed that everyone passes through a sequence of psychosocial stages that are genetically pre-determined. For a teenager, this constitutes identity versus role confusion. Significant changes occur over this time for an adolescent: from puberty (physical), through to socialisation into society and finally through the adolescent achieving a stronger sense of self-identity (psychological).

The rest of this section will concentrate on the developmental stages that affect a teenager.

## *Growing pains*

Puberty is one of the most rapid and dramatic periods of physical change in the human life cycle. Although parents and schools do a tremendous job of awareness raising, little can be done to prepare the young adolescent for the changes to come. From growth spurts and greater clumsiness to an increase in body hair, it can be a time of great insecurity for a teenager.

The rapid growth that the body experiences at this stage disturbs the previous trust in the body and mastery of its functions that were enjoyed in childhood (Erikson, 1959). For sexual maturity, the adolescent needs to 'grow into' their new body, which for a while may not feel comfortable. In addition, the hormones stimulating body growth and change are also working hard and can affect the teenager's emotions quite dramatically:

> . . . some days I'm way up and other days I'm way down, and the way I feel doesn't seem to have much to do with what's going on around me. It really scares me that I have these feelings that come from nowhere.
>
> (From survey conducted for Palmer and Puri, 2006)

These rapid rises in the level of sex hormones and fluctuations in other hormones are usually accompanied by irritability, moodiness, aggression and depression. However, with the vast majority of teenagers, the moodiness does pass with increasing age and confidence. However, low moods persist in some teenagers and they are diagnosed with depression. It is highly unusual for a child to become depressed but in the teenage years the frequency of depression does begin to rise (Klerman, 1988). The causes of teenage depression could be anything from a genetic predisposition or personality traits to crises of identity and difficulties in family relationships. Most people with depression deal with the unhelpful core beliefs that they are helpless or unlovable and these core beliefs may bring on depressive thoughts and emotions. Some studies have indicated that dealing with these automatic thoughts and unhelpful core beliefs (i.e. providing cognitive-behavioural therapy) is effective in assisting teenagers to overcome their depressed mood (Garber, 2009; Wethington et al., 2008).

## *The self-conscious teenager*

Teenagers' rapidly changing physical appearance can cause them to become much more self-conscious. They often start to hide themselves away, locking their bedroom doors or spending hours in the bathroom working on their appearance (White and Comininellis, 2006). The young teenager primps in front of the mirror or worries about acne. The hours spent in self-admiration or self-criticism tend to be directed towards impressing the audience that the young adolescent feels is always there.

Following fads appears to play an important role in achieving a positive self-image for a teenager. The teenager who looks and acts 'right' gains approval from friends. This is a time when self-image is paramount and teenagers work hard on creating an image they are comfortable with and, more importantly, one that is accepted by their peers (McCabe and Ricciardelli, 2001; Shroff and Thompson, 2006).

However, it is of concern that many eating disorders appear to start soon after puberty and persist through secondary school years (Mueller et al., 1995; Tiggemann et al., 1994). Research indicates that females are more likely than males to describe themselves as fat, to weigh themselves often and to diet frequently. They are also generally more dissatisfied with their physical appearance than are males (Cooper and Fairburn, 1983; Furnham and Calnan, 1998). Studies have also shown that body image dissatisfaction is more closely related to low self-esteem for girls than for boys (Furnam, Badmin and Sneade, 2002). This does not mean that boys have escaped the socio-cultural pressure to achieve the ideal figure, but that the desired outcomes are different.

Some research has indicated that males are more interested in their shape than weight, the ideal male body shape being a V-shaped figure with large biceps, chest and shoulders (Anderson and Di Domenico, 1992). Currently, there is little information on the impact, among males, of binge eating, excessive exercise or other behaviours associated with disturbed body image (Middleman, Vazquez and Durant, 1998; Moore, 1993). In addition to disturbed eating and exercise patterns, which may lead to significant health problems, males with a poor body image may develop psychological problems such as depression, low self-esteem and anxiety disorders (Braun et al., 1999).

Along with the obsession with physical appearance, adolescents may develop the notion that the 'world revolves around them' (Elkind, 1970). Teenagers show this egocentrism when they say that no-one has ever felt the way they do, suffered so much, loved so deeply or been so misunderstood.

Stuck in the middle of being a child and an adult, many teenagers get frustrated. Their bodies have developed adult capabilities, but the adult world is not ready to welcome them yet. This feeling of being in limbo can cause feelings of inadequacy and conflicts with siblings and parents, creating a level of teenage angst.

## Peer pressure

Peer pressure, both positive and negative, can be a powerful influence on teenagers. Friends are critical to a young person's emotional development. They provide a sense of security and feeling of belonging that can help teenagers make a successful transition to adulthood and independence.

However, when the group decision overrides individual creativity and independent thought, things can become more dangerous. This is often called 'groupthink' (Janis, 1972). Generally, motives for teenagers to conform to the opinion of the group include the desire to avoid being seen as foolish or to avoid embarrassing or angering other members of the group. On the downside, groupthink may cause groups to make hasty, irrational decisions where the individual teenagers' concerns are set aside, due to a fear of upsetting the group's balance. For this reason, they are particularly susceptible to 'do what everyone else is doing', even if it means participating in activities such as drinking, drugs or sex.

> At 16 I was not ready to lose my virginity, I didn't have a steady boyfriend and had little confidence in myself. I had no idea what I was getting myself in to. All my friends were having sex. They acted as if it was no big deal. It is! Trust me! I now know that I lost my virginity to the wrong guy he was a creep and I was just another girl to him.
>
> (From survey conducted for Palmer and Puri, 2006)

In addition, the influence of TV, movies, the internet and gaming encourage youth to experiment with drugs, alcohol and sex to a far greater extent than in earlier times. These pressures can cause enormous tension for youth. For example, 23% of 11- to 15-year-olds report drinking alcohol. Drinking becomes more common as young people move through their teenage years, rising to 45% of 15-year-olds (National Centre for Social Research/National Foundation for Educational Research, 2005).

Similarly, 18% of 11- to 15-year-olds have used drugs in the last year, most commonly cannabis. As with alcohol, cannabis use increases with age. An association between drug and alcohol use and unsafe sex has also been found: 20% of young men and 13% of young women aged 15–19 years cited alcohol as the main reason for first intercourse, and the younger the woman the more likely it is that alcohol was involved (Ingham, 2001).

However, research indicates that family relationships may have a greater link to anti-social behaviour than friends being a 'bad influence' on one another (Kearns and Forrest, 2000). Recent studies show that greater parental monitoring (knowing the whereabouts, activities and friends of one's child) can have a significant impact on a variety of adolescent outcomes, including anti-social behaviour such as drinking and smoking (Jacobson and Crockett, 2000; Ledoux et al., 2002).

## *The teenage identity*

The role of 'identity' in adolescent development is particularly important as teenagers begin to know and define themselves in ways that were not possible during their childhood. Identity is often described in terms of one's interpersonal characteristics, such as self-definition or personality traits, the roles and relationships one takes on in various interactions and one's personal values or moral beliefs.

It is during adolescence that teenagers may question their upbringing, religion, their parents' political beliefs and other values that they used to hold. They may begin to rebel against previously unquestioned norms, by refusing to go out with the family and possibly developing elaborate religious or political beliefs of their own. To quote Elkind (1970: 13), the adolescent is 'an impatient idealist, who believes that it is as easy to realise an ideal as it is to imagine it'. However, it is through questioning their current beliefs and the environment around them that they can decipher what fits in with the identity and image they are currently constructing. For Erikson (1968) a unitary sense of identity is created after a successful search for whom one is.

Other theories of adolescent development have suggested that teenagers will assume different perspectives according to the demands and constraints of a particular situation. Using this perspective the adolescent creates their self-image by assuming roles of others through playful stances that enable them to test out different facets of who they would like to become (Harter, 1998; Kihlstrom, 1993; McAdams, 1995).

For today's teenagers, the internet and advancing technologies have made this sort of role playing easier to conduct. The anonymity afforded to teenagers within virtual worlds allows more flexibility in safely exploring identity through language, role play and a persona they wish to assume. In a virtual world, you even get to construct your own body!

Research into current online environments, such as chat rooms, instant messaging and social networks, has revealed interesting trends in the way individual identity is presented, how language is used and the way interactions transpire

(Greenfield and Subrahmanyam, 2003; Herring, 2000). However, more research into this area is needed to have a comprehensive understanding of teenagers' 'online' persona and the impact this has on their 'offline' self-identity.

## The changing world of teenagers

A number of technological and sociological changes have taken place in recent years, many of which are likely to affect today's teenagers. From changing workforce demands, economic downturns, advances in technology and the changes in work–life patterns, the outlook for their future is very different from those even just a decade before them.

### *Education and entering the workforce*

Adolescents experience a number of changes in their social world, but perhaps the clearest social transition in early teenage years is the move from elementary to secondary school. The shift in the educational context is one of the first social markers of early adolescence (Elder, 1968) and has been characterised as one of the most potentially difficult. Eccles, Midgley and Adler (1984) indicated that adolescents are likely to endure greater difficulties during the middle school transition because of the increasingly negative relationship between students and teachers, changes in instructional practices and increasingly competitive marking practices and restrictions on the teenagers' autonomy. These social changes have also been used to explain the dip in self-esteem in early adolescents.

Although there is much research looking at the difficulties faced by those entering into adolescence, the social transition out of adolescence is perhaps less well understood (Donnellan, Trzesniewski and Robins, 2006). Unlike generations before, the teenagers of today face a very uncertain future. With neither further education nor taking on apprenticeships securing jobs, the youth of today are moving forward with great hesitation.

More than one in six young people leave school unable to read, write and add up properly, and the proportion of

16-year-olds staying on in full-time education in the UK is below the average for developed countries (Leitch Review of Skills, 2006).

Nearly one in five teenagers are now classed as 'Neet' – not in education, employment or training. According to figures from the Department for Children, Schools and Families (2009), 10.3% of school leavers aged 16–18 years were classed as Neets in 2008, which was up from 9.7% in 2007 and 8.9% a decade earlier. Among 18-year-olds alone, the figures reveal a massive jump, suggesting that more are leaving Sixth Form or further education colleges but then struggling to secure a job or university place.

Erikson (1968) suggested that the jobs people choose play a major role in their representation of themselves to the world. Research suggests that to be unemployed places a person outside the accepted, taken-for-granted system, setting them apart from those who are at work. Kelvin (1981) argues that the unemployed generally withdraw from much of their previous network of wider social activities, partly for financial reasons but also due to a subjective sense of inadequacy. In losing our job, we lose much of our social identity (Kelvin, 1981). Erikson (1968) claims that a state of acute identity confusion usually manifests itself at a time when the young person is faced with a combination of experiences that demand simultaneous commitment, including occupational choice. If this choice is denied to the school leaver, the opportunity to engage in other activities vital for development of a sense of personal identity may be denied as well. Failure to achieve an identity at this stage may prevent the development of intimacy (along with work, the other major criterion of adulthood).

Recessions and economic downturns can have a significant impact on young people entering into the workforce. Young people who are Neet are at greater risk of poor health and negative outcomes in later life. Being consistently jobless and without an income leaves many teenagers with a loss of social identity, low confidence and feelings of depression and isolation: 'Gutted. Depressed. Bored. Young people don't get given a chance' (Dear, 2009).

## The changing structure of the family unit

Family life in the UK has become much more diverse, with an increasing number of young people living in stepfamilies and one in four young people in lone-parent households (2001 UK Census). Furthermore, 80% of mothers of teenage children work, meaning that the majority of parents are juggling responsibilities at work and home. With most parents of children under 16 years working full time, and many couples moving away from their extended family, children spend less free time with either their parents or other relatives. Research has also shown that people in the UK work the longest hours in Europe, which affects the 'work–life balance' and the time parents spend with their children (4 Children Youth Review, 2006).

In these times of rapid social and technological changes, where there is a breakdown of many traditional values and beliefs (e.g. the nuclear family, women staying at home to look after children, etc.), it may be more difficult for young people to find continuity between what they have learnt and experienced as children and what they are learning and experiencing as teenagers. This may lead them to experiment with several types of identities, some possibly more extreme than others, whilst trying to 'find themselves' (Elkind, 1970; Erikson, 1968).

## Technology – the way teenagers communicate

Technology now plays a huge part in teenage lives, with 87% of teenagers aged 12–17 years using the internet and 75% of online teenagers preferring instant messaging to regular email. An overwhelming majority of teenagers (84%) report owning at least one personal media device: a desktop or laptop computer, a mobile phone or a Personal Digital Assistant (PDA) (Lenhart, Madden and Hitlin, 2005).

There is no doubt that digital technology is changing the way we all think, but for those brought up in this technological age it is the only way they know. New phrases such as 'toxic childhood' re-emphasise concern with the prominence of technology in children's lives. Current research indicates that children spend 6 hours a day in front of a TV, computer or game console. Although alarming, it is not surprising to hear that one in three children feel that the computer is the single thing they could not live without! (Childwise, 2009).

## Social networking

Social networking sites are gaining popularity by the day. Facebook is currently the fourth largest site in the world with 340 million unique visitors (Common Sense Media, 2009), trailing only Google, Microsoft and Yahoo sites. However, the popularity of social networking sites has caused a furore with some experts, indicating that these sites may change children's brains, resulting in 'short attention spans, sensationalism, inability to empathise and a shaky sense of identity' (Wintour, 2009).

A national poll of teenagers and parents on social networking behaviour in America (Common Sense Media White Paper, 2009) indicated that children are increasingly connecting with friends, classmates and people with similar interests through social networks, and that parents were out of the loop. Social networks and mobile communication connect children to their friends 24/7. Conversations that start in school may well continue in the virtual world when at home. Teenagers are using social networking to share information, make connections and develop their identities in new ways.

However, the anonymity of the web can create a false sense of security, with over a quarter (28%) of the surveyed teenagers indicating that they shared personal information they normally would not have shared in public, and a further 39% indicating that they had posted something they regretted. What is more concerning is that a quarter of respondents indicated that they had shared a profile with a false identity.

Where teenagers communicate anonymously or through a disguised identity there tends to be a reduction in the perception of the accountability of their actions, and this is how irresponsible behaviours such as cyber bullying become a reality. Eighteen per cent of teenagers say that someone has posted a humiliating picture of them or humiliated them online.

The picture of the impact of social networking sites is far from clear. Although benefits of using network sites are apparent – they give young people freedom and responsibility for the way they communicate, entertain themselves and obtain knowledge (see Becta, 2008) – research into the long-term psychological impact of this type of communication is still in its infancy.

## Texting

The average number of texts per phone user is 357 per month but that number jumps to 1742 for teenagers aged 13–17 years, who text more than any other age group (Covey, 2008). This has raised concerns about increased levels of anxiety, distraction at school, falling school grades, sleep deprivation and repetitive stress injury. With 95% of 16-year-olds having their own mobile phones, it looks unlikely that this trend is going to pass.

However, it is not all doom and gloom. A recent report carried out by Samsung Telecommunications America (2008) revealed that text messaging has broadened the lines of communication for many parents and teens, with over half of those reporting that it had actually improved their relationship. The survey suggests that more parent–teenage communication is being conducted by text and over half of all teenagers aged 13–19 years report that they now communicate more often with their parents since they began text messaging.

## Additional pressures that teenagers may face

As if being a teenager was not hard enough work, it is important to bear in mind that along with becoming a teenager, other issues or concerns do not disappear. Whether this be a disability, belonging to a minority ethnic background or dealing with parents getting a divorce (just over half of all divorces in the UK have at least one child aged less than 16 years: Office for National Statistics, 2006), teenagers may find themselves feeling isolated and unsure of how to deal with these changes in addition to those most commonly associated with adolescence.

The teenage years are a time when many young people begin to redefine themselves and become more articulate in what they think of the relationships around them (especially with those of authority over the teenager). It is also when they become more able to express their own feelings (of sexual identity or of their own belief systems). This is not always easy to do and a teenager may find opposition and rejection in doing so.

## Coaching and mentoring teenagers

Coaching adolescents through the teenage years is not new. This psychosocial development stage of identity versus role confusion (Erikson, 1965) is a time when adolescents are concerned about how they appear to others and what they perceive themselves to be. As we know, young people struggle to belong and to be accepted and affirmed while at the same time working towards becoming individuals in their own right. The confusion, mixed in with expectations (of themselves and others), can lead to isolation, vulnerability and depression.

Twenty years ago depression in children was almost unknown (or at least not recognised) but now the fastest rate of increase in depression is among young people (Yapko, 2009). Fortunately, researchers who analysed dozens of studies on cognitive-behavioural therapy (CBT) have concluded that the technique is an effective means of reducing symptoms related to depression, anxiety and post-traumatic stress disorder in teenagers and adolescents who have experienced some type of trauma (Wethington et al., 2008). In addition to relieving current symptoms, CBT and other traditional coaching techniques also appear to be an effective means of reducing the likelihood that a struggling young person will engage in additional dangerous behaviour later on in life.

Research has also highlighted that teenagers can be more receptive to self-help techniques compared to traditional coaching techniques (Stice et al., 2007). One possible explanation for this is that teenagers are less enthusiastic about having face-to-face coaching sessions (they tend to have a higher drop-out rate). One effective way of dealing with this has been via mentoring.

Support via the internet and via social networking sites is usually well received, as are mentoring sessions based on life skills such as time management or assertion. In addition, there has been strong empirical evidence to support parent management training for teenagers (Kazdin and Weisz, 1998) – where parent management training refers to procedures in which parents are trained to alter their child's behaviour at home. This approach is based on the general view that conduct problems are inadvertently developed and sustained in the home by maladaptive parent–child interactions.

New mentoring websites are also becoming more acceptable and popular (e.g. horsesmouth.co.uk) but there is some concern that people are not necessarily receiving 'professional expert advice' through these websites because people volunteer themselves onto the website to offer help and advice in areas they subjectively feel they have expertise in. However, this is made quite clear in the explanation of what is on offer. This type of mentoring does appear to be quite altruistic in nature for both the user and the 'expert', thus having great 'feel good' appeal.

## Case study

Paul was a shy 18-year-old who was diagnosed with depression. He had recently moved from Leeds to London, where he had started university.

Paul had come from a small suburb in Leeds, having known most of his friends from childhood. Before joining university Paul had broken up with his long-term girlfriend, as he did not feel that a long-distance relationship could work.

At university Paul had made very few friends, confining himself to his room on most evenings, smoking and mainly eating takeaways. He was finding that attending university lectures became harder and harder and was struggling with completing assignments on time.

Paul expressed concern that he did not 'fit in' to his new environment. Although he was enjoying the course, 'student life' was not at all what he expected. He admitted that he found it hard to make friends, as it had been so long since he had needed to. He felt self-conscious and worried that no-one would like him. He also expressed concern that he had left it too late and people had already made their social groups.

Paul was thinking of quitting university, as he could not cope with the isolation and was missing his girlfriend too much. A number of coaching sessions were set up for Paul. The coaching sessions initially helped him to elicit his hot cognitions relating to why he had not been able to make friends with his new university colleagues (they wouldn't like me, I'm not that cool, they're too smart) and to dispute them (e.g. if I wasn't that smart, I wouldn't be at university with them). It was also used to tackle issues of low self-esteem (I don't belong anywhere, no-one likes me, I'm pathetic), where his negative thoughts were questioned and a more realistic attitude developed.

Coaching sessions were also used for goal setting, as Paul was finding the lack of structure at university quite disconcerting. By doing this, Paul was able to put things back into perspective, bearing in mind his initial motivations for coming to university. In later sessions Paul worked on assertion techniques, which assisted with his lack of confidence.

Further university mentoring courses were suggested for Paul, including time management (to structure his day in the most productive manner) and cookery classes to expand his current culinary abilities. Other self-help materials were also given to Paul for these aspects (e.g. books/articles on mind mapping, relaxation techniques and smoking cessation).

Paul found that coaching enabled him to see the 'wood from the trees' and that most of the problems he was having were out of fear of the unknown, rather than a genuine dislike for university.

Paul had started going out a lot more and found that he could discuss many of his concerns about coursework with fellow students (and that they had very similar thoughts on the lack of structure as he did!). He also 'made up' with his ex-girlfriend, after realising through the coaching that he was missing their relationship too much and that it was OK to be homesick!

Paul also found that mentoring via structured group sessions and self-help books had helped with time management, relaxation and positivity but he was still eating out and smoking too much. However, he put this down to the lifestyle he was choosing to lead rather than being due to depression or anxiety.

## Discussion issues

1 Are social networking sites hindering teenagers' abilities to create meaningful relationships outside the virtual world?
2 Should more coaches move towards online coaching when working with teenagers?
3 Do today's teenagers have more to be stressed about than previous generations?
4 How can the anonymity of the web create a false sense of security for young people?

## References

4 Children Youth Review (2006) *An Enquiry into the Offer to Young People in the UK Today.* Retrieved from http://www.4children. org.uk/uploads/information/1MS_YouthReview_Inquiry_leaflet. pdf on 31 January 2010.

Anderson, A. E. and Di Domenico, L. (1992) Diet vs shape content of popular male and female magazines: A dose response relationship to the incidence of eating disorders. *International Journal of Eating Disorders, 11*: 283–287.

Arnett, J. J. (2000) Emerging adulthood: A theory of development from the late teens through the twenties. *American Psychologist, 55*: 469–480.

Becta (2008) *Harnessing Technology Review 2008: The Role of Technology and Its Impact on Education.* (Full Report.) Coventry: Becta.

Braun, D. L., Sunday, S. R., Huang, A. and Halmi, K. A. (1999) More males seek treatment for eating disorders. *International Journal for Eating Disorders, 20*: 415–424.

Childwise (2009) *Childwise Monitor Report 2008/09*. Retrieved from www.childwise.co.uk/Childwise-monitor-survey.asp on 8 August 2009.

Christie, D. and Viner, R. (2005) ABC of adolescence: Adolescent development. *British Medical Journal, 330*: 301–304.

Common Sense Media (2009) *Social Networks and Teen Lives*. San Francisco, CA: The Benenson Strategy Group.

Common Sense Media White Paper (2009) *Digital Literacy and Citizenship in the 21st Century: Educating, Empowering and Protecting America's Kids*. San Francisco, CA: The Benenson Strategy Group.

Cooper, P. J. and Fairburn, C. G. (1983) Binge eating and self-induced vomiting in the community: A preliminary study. *British Journal of Psychiatry, 142*: 139–144.

Covey, N. (2008) *Nielsen Mobile Report: Flying Fingers*. Nielsen Telecom Practice Group. Retrieved from http://en-us.nielsen.com/main/insights/consumer_insight/issue_12/flying_fingers on 16 January 2010.

Dear, P. (2009) *Working, What's the Point?* BBC News. Retrieved from http://news.bbc.co.uk/1/hi/magazine/7816500.stm on 12 August 2009.

Department for Children, Schools and Families (2009) *14–19 Reform: 16–18 year old NEETS*. Retrieved from www.dcsf.gov.uk/14–19 on 16 August 2009.

Donnellan, M. B., Trzesniewski, K. H. and Robins, R. W (2006) Personality and self-esteem development in adolescence. In T. Mroczek and T. Little (Eds.), *Handbook of Personality Development* (pp. 285–309). Hillsdale, NJ: Lawrence Erlbaum Associates, Inc.

Eccles, J. S., Midgley, C. and Adler, T. (1984) Grade-related changes in the school environment: Effects on achievement motivation. In J. G. Nicholls (Ed.), *The Development of Achievement Motivation* (pp. 283–331). Greenwich, CT: JAI Press.

Elder, G. H. (1968) The challenge of life course studies: Bringing context to human development. *Educational Review, 37*: 594–619.

Elkind, D. (1970) Erik Erikson's eight stages of man. *New York Times Magazine* (http://ceed.pdx.edu/ectc_sscbt/pdfs/EriksonsEightAgesofMan.pdf).

Erikson, E. H. (1950) *Childhood and Society*. New York: Norton.

Erikson, E. H. (1959) *Identity and the Life Cycle*. New York: International Universities Press.

Erikson, E. H. (1965) *Childhood and Society*. Harmondsworth, Middlesex: Penguin.

Erikson, E. H. (1968) *Identity: Youth and Crisis*. New York: Norton.

Freud, S. (1977) *Three Essays on the Theory of Sexuality*. Pelican Freud Library. Harmondsworth, Middlesex: Penguin. (Original work published 1905.)

Furnham, A. and Calnan, A. (1998) Eating disturbances, self-esteem, reasons for exercising and body weight dissatisfaction in adolescent males. *European Eating Disorders Review*, *6*: 58–72.

Furnham, A., Badmin, N. and Sneade, I. (2002) Body image dissatisfaction: Gender differences in eating attitudes, self-esteem, and reasons for exercise. *Journal of Psychology*, *136*: 581–596.

Garber, J. (2009) Prevention of depression in at-risk adolescents: A randomised control trial. *Journal of the American Medical Association*, *301*: 2215–2224.

Greenfield, P. M. and Subrahmanyam, K. (2003) Online discourse in a teen chatroom: New codes and new modes of coherence in a visual medium. *Applied Developmental Psychology*, *24*: 713–738.

Harter, S. (1998) The development of self-representations. In W. Damon (Ed.), *Handbook of Child Psychology, Social Emotional and Personality Development* (6th ed., pp. 553–617). New York: Wiley.

Herring, S. C. (2000) Gender differences in CMC: Findings and implications. *Computer Professionals for Social Responsibilty Newsletter*, *18*(1).

Ingham, R. (2001) *Survey Commissioned by Channel Four for the Series 'Generation Sex'*. Retrieved from www.channel4.com. on 15 September 2009.

Jacobson, K. C. and Crockett, L. J. (2000) Parental monitoring and adolescent adjustment: An ecological perspective. *Journal of Research on Adolescence*, *10*: 65–97.

Janis, I. L. (1972) *Victims of Groupthink*. Boston, MA: Houghton Mifflin Company.

Kazdin, A. E. and Weisz, J. R. (1998) Identifying and developing empirically supported child and adolescent treatments. *Journal of Consulting and Clinical Psychology*, *66*: 19–36.

Kearns, A. and Forrest, R. (2000) Social cohesion and multi-level urban governance. *Urban Studies*, *37*: 995–1017.

Kelvin, P. (1981) Work as a source of identity. *British Journal of Guidance and Counselling*, *9*: 2–11.

Kihlstrom, J. F. (1993) The continuum of consciousness. *Consciousness and Cognition*, *2*: 334–354.

Klerman, G. L. (1988) The current age of youthful melancholia: Evidence for increase in depression among adolescents and young adults. *British Journal of Psychiatry*, *152*: 4–14.

Ledoux, S., Miller, P., Choquet, M. and Plant, M. (2002) Family structure, parent–child relationships and alcohol and other drug use amongst teenagers in France and the United Kingdom. *Alcohol and Alcoholism*, *37*: 52–60.

Leitch Review of Skills (2006) *Prosperity for All in the Global Economy – World Class Skills*. London: HM Treasury.

Lenhart, A., Madden, M. and Hitlin, P. (2005) *Teens and Technology: Youth are Leading the Transition to a Fully Wired and Mobile Nation*. Washington, DC: Pew Internet and American Life Project.

McAdams, D. P. (1995) What do we know when we know a person? *Journal of Personality*, *63*: 365–696.

McCabe, M. P. and Ricciardelli, L. A. (2001) Parent, peer, and media influences on body image and strategies to both increase and decrease body size among adolescent boys and girls. *Adolescence*, *36*: 225–240.

Middleman, A. B., Vazquez, I. and Durant, R. H. (1998) Eating patterns, physical activity, and attempts to change weight among adolescents. *Journal of Adolescent Health*, *22*: 37–42.

Moore, D. C. (1993) Body image and eating behaviours in adolescents. *Journal of the American College of Nutrition*, *12*: 505–510.

Mueller, C., Field, T., Yando, R., Harding, J., Gonzalez, K., Lasko, D., et al. (1995) Undereating and overeating concerns among adolescents. *Journal of Child Psychology and Psychiatry*, *36*: 1019–1025.

National Centre for Social Research/National Foundation for Educational Research (2005) *Drug Use, Smoking and Drinking among Young People in England in 2004*. London: National Statistics/NHS Health and Social Care Information Centre.

Office for National Statistics (2006) *Marriage, Divorce and Adoption Statistics – Series FM2*. London: ONS.

Palmer, S. and Puri, A. (2006) *Coping with Stress at University: A Survival Guide*. London: Sage.

Piaget, J. (1972) Intellectual evolution from adolescence to adulthood. *Human Development*, *15*: 1–21.

Samsung Telecommunications America (2008) *Mobile Matters Survey: How Text Messaging Improves the Parent–Teen Relationships*. New York: Kelton Research.

Santrock, J. W. (2008) A *Topical Approach to Life Span Development*. New York: McGraw-Hill.

Shroff, H. and Thompson, K. J. (2006) Peer influences, body-image dissatisfaction, eating dysfunction and self-esteem in adolescent girls. *Journal of Health Psychology*, *11*: 533–551.

Stice, E., Burton, E., Bearman, S. K. and Rohde, P. (2007) Randomized trial of a brief depression prevention program: An elusive search for a psychosocial placebo control condition. *Behaviour Research and Therapy*, *45*: 863–876.

Tiggemann, M., Winefield, H., Winefield, A. and Goldney, R. (1994) Gender differences in the psychological correlates of body weight in young adults. *Psychology and Health*, *9*: 395–451.

Wethington, H. R., Hahn, R. A., Fuqua-Whitley, D. S., Sipe, T. A., Crosby, A. E., Johnson, R. L. et al. (2008) The effectiveness of interventions to reduce psychological harm from traumatic events among children and adolescents: A systematic review. *American Journal of Preventive Medicine*, 35: 287–313.

White, J. and Comininellis, N. (2006) *Nine Things Teens Should Know and Parents Are Afraid to Talk About*. Washington, DC: New Leaf Press.

Wintour, P. (2009) *Facebook and Bebo Risk 'Infantalising' the Human Mind*. Retrieved from www.guardian.co.uk on 4 August 2009.

Yapko, M. D. (2009) Major depression in preschool children? *Psychology Today*. Retrieved from www.psychologytoday.com on 8 August 2009.

## Recommended reading

Palmer, S. (2006) *Toxic Childhood*. London: Orion Publishers.

Palmer, S. and Puri, A. (2006) *Coping with Stress at University: A Survival Guide*. London: Sage.

# 4

# From twenties to thirties

## Sheila Panchal

This chapter will focus on two key transition points that occur within early adulthood. The first will be termed the 'early 20s' transition throughout, which often represents the shift from the academic to the working world, typically leaving college or university, in the 21–24-year age range. The second is the 'turning 30' transition, which concerns those in the 25–35-year age group. These two distinct transition points have been identified as key developmental turning points (e.g. Levinson, 1986) and are influenced by today's social and cultural landscape. In the popular literature, both of these transition points have been referred to as the 'quarter-life crisis' (Barr, 2004; Robbins and Wilner, 2001), implying a reflection point in the same vein as the mid-life crisis. A Common Purpose (1994) report indicated that 83% of respondents believe that there is such a thing as the quarter-life crisis, where they and their peers think about what they want from life. However, other research challenges these views: for example, Dunn and Merriam (1995) found no persuasive evidence for Levinson's 'Age-Thirty Transition' in a large sample of adults.

The essence of the 'early 20s' transition can often be seen in terms of dealing with the challenges of adapting to the 'real world' following the relatively structured academic world. It is characterised by greater independence and therefore responsibility for career, finances, relationships and lifestyle. As this transition is resolved, individuals tend to experience a period of stability during their 20s. The 'turning

30' transition follows. After the exploratory and relatively present-focused lifestyle of the 20s, individuals may reflect on their experiences and seriously consider their long-term future and commitments for the first time. 'Turning 30' questions include 'who am I?' and 'what do I want for my future'.

Both transitions are opportunities for self-development and growth. They are characterised by self-reflection as individuals take stock of their past and consider their future. There can be a feeling of being 'in limbo' between two different phases of life. If the transitions are not negotiated positively, individuals can become 'stuck' and experience emotional and physical symptoms, or turn to escapist coping behaviours such as excessive socialising or travel (Panchal and Jackson, 2005).

Research suggests that there are positive links between optimum developmental experiences in early adulthood and later development (e.g. Roisman et al., 2004). This implies that a positive 'early 20s' transition is likely to set the scene for a smooth 'turning 30' and later transitions such as midlife and retirement. A positive course for the future is likely to be set if the 'early 20s' transition results in high self-awareness and a sense of purpose. Coaching can be helpful in achieving this goal.

Today's cultural and social setting also affects how these transitions are experienced. Today's generation of 20- and 30-somethings are collectively known as 'Generation Y' (e.g. Eisner, 2005) and generational factors will be discussed. Cross-cultural beliefs and values are likely to affect people; for example, Western cultures tend to support the concept of an extended adolescence where people have an exploratory period into their 20s and do not tend to make longer-term choices until 30 approaches (Arnett, 2000). Previous generations in Western cultures and other cultures today have greater expectations that career, relationship and family commitments are made in the early 20s, which affects the transitional experience. This chapter will largely focus on the experiences of 20- and 30-somethings in current Western culture.

As with all transition points and generational factors, it is important to avoid generalising, stereotyping and labelling. This chapter aims to offer insights from psychology and other disciplines that may provide useful context for coaches working with those in their 20s and 30s.

## About Generation Y

Psychological research pertaining to both transitions will be reviewed separately, however there are generational factors common to both transitions.

Paul Redmond (2009) from the University of Liverpool cites social factors shaping Generation Y. Technological change is a major factor, as is the change in institutions, as organisations are more dynamic than before. He also states that this generation has been cared for and protected by their Baby Boomer 'helicopter' parents more so than any other. As a result, Generation Y are confident and entrepreneurial, and want a good work–life balance.

Generation Y have grown up in a society where there are significantly more choices than for previous generations, with the advent of world travel, far-reaching technological advances and greater social mobility than ever before. Redmond (2009) refers to the 3 Cs of 'Change', 'Challenge' and 'Choice'. A positive outcome of greater choice is greater opportunity. However, choice may bring pressure. Schwartz (2003) states that choice overload can lead to questioning of decisions even before they are made, create unrealistically high expectations and promote self-blame for any failures. Extensive choice can be overwhelming and people can be unsure which way to turn. When making decisions about their place in society during the 'early 20s' and 'turning 30' transitions, people can become paralysed by the challenge of finding the right and best answer among endless options.

In addition, there are greater expectations placed on today's generation than ever before. Media and celebrity culture demonstrate that fame and wealth are on offer and there is nothing stopping individuals having it all from a young age. A US study by the Pew Research Center (2007) indicates that fame and fortune are important goals for this generation, with 8 out of 10 saying that getting rich is the most, or second most, important goal in their lives. Expectations also come from parents, who tend to measure their children by a life gauge appropriate to Baby Boomers as opposed to Generation Y (Panchal and Jackson, 2007). Therefore they expect a steady job, marriage and children as 30 approaches. Added to this are expectations from peers, who have chosen particular routes in life and are seeking confirmation by encouraging others to follow. Social and familial expectations can be exacerbated for those from dual-culture backgrounds.

The flipside of social mobility is the breakdown of many traditional support networks, such as religion, community and extended families. This can affect people's experiences of transitions. Information and communications technology has widened the communities that we can be part of but has reduced the depth of commitment that we feel towards or from those networks (Gergen, 1991). Those experiencing the 'early 20s' and 'turning 30' transitions are often left to deal with their personal challenges without the emotional and practical support that they need. The use of social networking sites such as Facebook is second nature for Generation Y. The Pew report cited that 54% of participants had used one or more of these sites. This has the advantage of helping them maintain networks that otherwise may be lost but the disadvantage of compromising the quality of relationships as virtual communication takes precedence over face-to-face communication.

Finally, Generation Y have been raised in a healthy economic climate and have enjoyed the benefits of prosperity as children and teenagers. The current financial uncertainty may also affect their experience of transitions. Eisner (2005) noted that Generation Y were raised in a time of economic prosperity but are coming of age in an era of economic uncertainty and violence, such as 9/11. As a result, they value home and family and are keen to meet their personal as well as career goals. For some, high expectations of 'having it all' may lead to difficult transitions as they face the reality of the current economic climate. Furnham (2008) observes generational differences in financial attitudes, noting that Generation Y are materialistic and security conscious, dependent on parents for longer and used to long-term debt.

The idea of a 20-something crisis point has also pervaded popular culture. For example, in *Generation X: Tales for an Accelerated Culture* by Douglas Coupland (1991), a 'mid-twenties breakdown' is described as 'a period of mental collapse occurring in one's twenties, often caused by an inability to function outside of school or structured environments, coupled with a realisation of one's essential aloneness in the world' (p. 27).

## 'Early 20s' transition

Levinson (1986: 7) described the 'early 20s' transition as a 'developmental bridge between pre-adulthood and early adulthood'. It is about truly stepping into adult life, experiencing emotional and financial independence from the family of origin for the first time and adapting to the associated freedom and responsibility. Today's Generation Y 20-somethings have been raised by the Baby Boomer generation in a relatively prosperous economic climate and yet face uncertain economic times as adults.

The 'early 20s' turning point presents opportunities and challenges in different life areas. It is a time when individuals tend to start their careers, embarking on an initial path. Although early career choices may have been made previously, at this point they are being reviewed and acted upon. There are challenges associated with making choices and finding a job in line with them. The plethora of choice in conjunction with a competitive job market can be tough, particularly for graduates who are feeling the pressure of university debt to pay off. The other major 'early 20s' career challenge is adapting to the working world. Working environments operate by different rules than academic ones, and are far less structured. Some thrive and others struggle. Most are familiar with the clear goals and feedback of formal education and take time to adapt to the ambiguity and politics of organisations.

Generation Y tend to have high expectations of careers. Research shows that they are looking for more than money, citing meaningful work, flexibility, quick progression and work–life balance as important factors. A CIPD (2008) report cited key Generation Y career needs as personal development, team work, challenge and life/work balance. Given that they have grown up in an environment of security (cared for by their Baby Boomer parents) and choice, they will move from organisations if their needs are not met. They may have seen their Baby Boomer parents experience organisational downsizing, so they may not have expectations of a 'job for life'. Some will find their route to getting their needs met. Others may find that their expectations are not in line with organisations that are managed by Generation X and Baby Boomers who started off making the tea and expect young workers to do the same. Either way, the 'early 20s' transition could be characterised by job and career changes as people explore and experiment. In 1975, those under 25 years old could expect to be in their second job. By the 1990s they would expect to be in their fourth (Fox, 2005).

Relationships are also evaluated during the 'early 20s' transition. Erikson (1950) describes the task of young adulthood as 'intimacy vs isolation' and the early 20s as a time when this is starting to be explored. Individuals may be grappling with the complexities of intimate relationships. Relationships established at college may be evaluated and fail to survive the transition, as careers and other interests take priority. Similarly, friendship groups may change as people move to new places with work, or take time to travel. Some may maintain their social network, or quickly establish a new one. Others may feel isolated as friends take different paths. Those who positively deal with the transition will find themselves enjoying their new lifestyle, yet some will look back and yearn for the stability and familiarity of their college or university life.

Finances come to the fore as part of the 'early 20s' transition. Some Generation Y individuals will enter the working world with significant student debt, and experience pressure to pay it off. The Push Student Debt Survey (2009) indicates that students starting university in 2009 can expect to owe £23,500 upon graduation. People earn for the first time and face the task of managing their money.

## 'Turning 30' transition

The 'turning 30' transition is characterised by considering deeper commitments to work, relationships and lifestyle. According to Levinson (1986) a period of stability follows the 'early 20s' transition where an initial life structure is established and maintained. Individuals start to work, develop relationships and find their feet as adults. As 30 approaches, transition begins again. Life choices made to date are re-evaluated in the light of the future. Decisions made in the early 20s may not fit any more. It is a time when questions about personal identity lead to a deeper sense of self. Changes are made in preparation for the second adult 'life structure' in the early 30s where deeper commitments to work and relationships tend to be made and there is a greater self-understanding and value. Reinke, Holmes and Harris (1985) studied a sample of middle-class American women and found that three-quarters indicated they started a period of major psychosocial adjustment between the ages of 27 and 30 years.

Research by Panchal and Jackson (2007) suggests that during the 'turning 30' transition some individuals focus on the future for the first time in their lives. There is a sense of being 'in limbo' between a familiar past and an uncertain future, which can feel unsettling:

In my early 20s I didn't feel any pressure to settle down to a career and a steady home life. I loved my life and happily travelled. Now, in my late 20s, I'm a bit anxious about getting older, without savings, a decent job and not much consideration for my future.[1]

I feel like I got lost in my 20s. I spent all my time running away from the pressure of expectation, chasing a hedonistic lifestyle of drinking and socialising. I guess I realised that it can't go on forever. I needed to face up to my personal responsibilities and this meant I had to get to know myself again, to establish a sense of myself as an adult. Am I the same person as I was when I left university? Do I want the same things? I don't know yet. They're tough questions.[1]

Gould (1978) states that between ages 28 and 34, individuals 'open up to what's inside'. They face up to the false assumption that life is simple and controllable. People start to think about what they do, and why. There is a need to find a sense of purpose, to understand values, to be confident and to trust one's own judgement. There is a search for a sense of self. Life events theory (Holmes and Rahe, 1967) also applies to 'turning 30', as for today's generation a cluster of significant life events tends to occur at this time, such as marriage, parenthood, buying a house and potentially parental illness or loss of parents.

Journalist Gail Sheehy (1976) shared a theory of adult development in her popular book *Passages*, building on psychological theories. She describes the 'trying 20s' as a relatively stable time when people are aiming to settle into adulthood and are trying different careers, partners and life paths in order to find a fit with what they 'should' be doing. In the late 20s or early 30s, people tend to experience a 'Catch-30' where these choices do not seem to fit any more. The emphasis moves from 'what should I do?' to 'what do I want?'. Sheehy believes that people make life changes at this stage and life stabilises once again in the early 30s. In an updated version of the theory, Sheehy (1995) says that longer life expectancy is affecting developmental paths, so that adolescence is prolonged until 30 and people do not feel fully grown up until they are in their 40s. Therefore 40 represents what 30 used to represent.

Panchal and Jackson (2007) highlight some challenges that arise during 'turning 30' transitions. As people review their careers, they may feel the need to change and settle on a path that they are happy with. This can be challenging if they have committed the last 10 years to one path and now want to switch. Alternatively, individuals can find themselves 'stuck' at a certain level and keen to move forwards within their profession or organisation. A desire to raise status or earn more money can create a sense of urgency. Another common issue is that of work–life balance. People can find that they are devoting their lives to work as they climb the corporate ladder and struggle to juggle other priorities in their lives. A Common Purpose (2004) report noted that 59% of young people are looking for something more from their jobs and the optimum age for career disillusionment is 30.

Relationships are key during the 'turning 30' transition. Office for National Statistics (2009a) data for England and Wales shows that the average age of first marriage is 31.9 years for men and 29.8 years for women. Those who are single may start focusing on finding a partner. Their single status can become a source of concern as others 'settle down'. This can be enhanced for women, who become increasingly aware of their biological clock. Current relationships are reviewed for long-term potential rather than for right now. They may end as individuals take stock and decide that their current partner does not have a place in their future. Common life events include first-time co-habitation, buying property as a couple and marriage. With them come questions about commitment as individuals grapple with the challenges of balancing intimacy with independence, as per Erikson's (1950s) challenge of young adulthood.

Successful resolution of the 'early 20s' transition tends to result in financial and emotional independence from parents. As part of the 'turning 30' transition, relationships with parents change again. Parents are getting older and there can be greater concern about their health and emphasis on taking care of them. Many become, or consider becoming, parents themselves. In 2008 the mean age of women giving birth was 29.3 years (Office for National Statistics, 2009b). This signifies emotional and lifestyle changes (see Chapter 6).

Friendship groups that may have become established pre or post the 'early 20s' transition can change, as friends take different directions with their lives, such as marriage or parenthood, or people move to different places. There can be a risk of social isolation. Others can find themselves struggling with the demands of the many friendships and acquaintances that they have gathered during their 20s.

People may place greater emphasis on their health. Signs of ageing become evident for the first time so health can become a more prominent concern. There can be a sense of being 'in limbo' from a social and leisure perspective, as the activities associated with the 20s may no longer be engaging.

Paying attention to finances can become increasingly important, given the new focus on the future associated with the 'turning 30' transition. People are facing the financial responsibilities of home ownership, children and old age.

Gender differences can become more prominent during the 'turning 30' transition than during the 'early 20s' transition due to the impact of the biological clock. Technological advances mean that procedures such as egg freezing can prolong a woman's fertility, yet overall women are affected by declining fertility in their 30s and feel pressure to make decisions in order to have a family.

See Figure 4.1 on page 81 for a model of 'turning 30' transitions (Panchal and Jackson, 2007).

## Coaching

Early adulthood transitions are opportunities for transformational growth and development. However, individuals can become 'stuck' during these life phases and display negative emotional and behavioural responses (Panchal and Jackson, 2007). They can commonly feel 'out of control' or that 'things don't feel quite right'. The emotional experience can range from a mild sense of confusion to more serious anxiety or depression. The more serious emotional responses can be caused by excessive rumination either individually or with friends who share similar feelings.

Behavioural responses are focused on escape strategies such as unplanned, significant life change or avoidance behaviour. Individuals leave jobs or relationships in an attempt to fulfil the need to make change in their lives. Travelling is another common response. Increased drug and alcohol use provide a way to escape from the difficult questions that individuals are beginning to ask themselves about their identity and future. Alternative behaviours include making significant life decisions and commitments solely due to time pressures, such as marriage or career acceleration.

Coaching is an effective mechanism for facilitating positive 20- and 30-something transitions. One of the key aspects

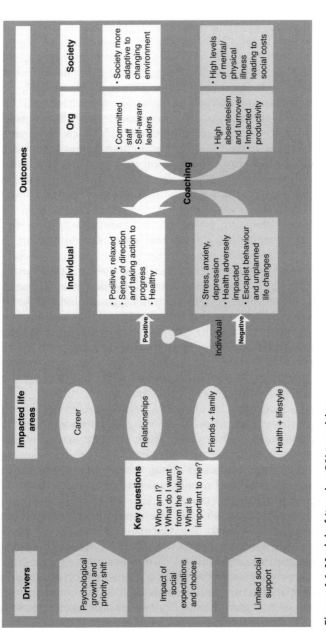

*Figure 4.1* Model of 'turning 30' transitions

of coaching is to promote self-awareness so that the Generation Y individual is able to make effective choices from the sea of options available to them in all areas of life. A coaching model for 'turning 30' has been developed by Panchal and Jackson (2007) – see Figure 4.2 on page 83.

Surfacing and discussing external expectations can be a useful part of the coaching process, as can developing a vision for the future. A shorter-term focus may be more useful for the 'early 20s' transition and a longer-term vision for 'turning 30'. Solution-focused and positive psychology approaches offer useful tools to facilitate insights and progress. Supporting an individual at this stage is likely to help with future transitions. For example, a carefully considered career decision based on self-awareness rather than external expectations during the 'early 20s' transition can prevent a 'turning 30' career crisis.

Another key element of coaching through these transitional points is to consider transitions as a normal part of healthy development. This addresses the unhelpful beliefs that many hold during this time: that everyone else has their life 'sorted' and they are alone in their questioning and uncertainty. Often, if they do share their feelings with friends, the result is shared rumination rather than constructive problem-solving. A coach can act as a trusted, independent advisor and encourage a solution focus.

Organisations can benefit from considering how to support their Generation Y individuals. By considering the needs and values of younger workers they are creating a competitive advantage in the war for talent. Through educating their top talent about transitions, organisations can prevent potential derailment and encourage the retention of their future leaders.

Carefully designed graduate development programmes will consider the 'early 20s' transition issues facing graduates starting work, as well as the specific needs of this particular generation of graduates. Typical graduate programmes focus largely on technical skills without paying attention to the interpersonal and self-management skills that are critical for success in organisations. These capabilities include areas such as career planning, stress management, communication,

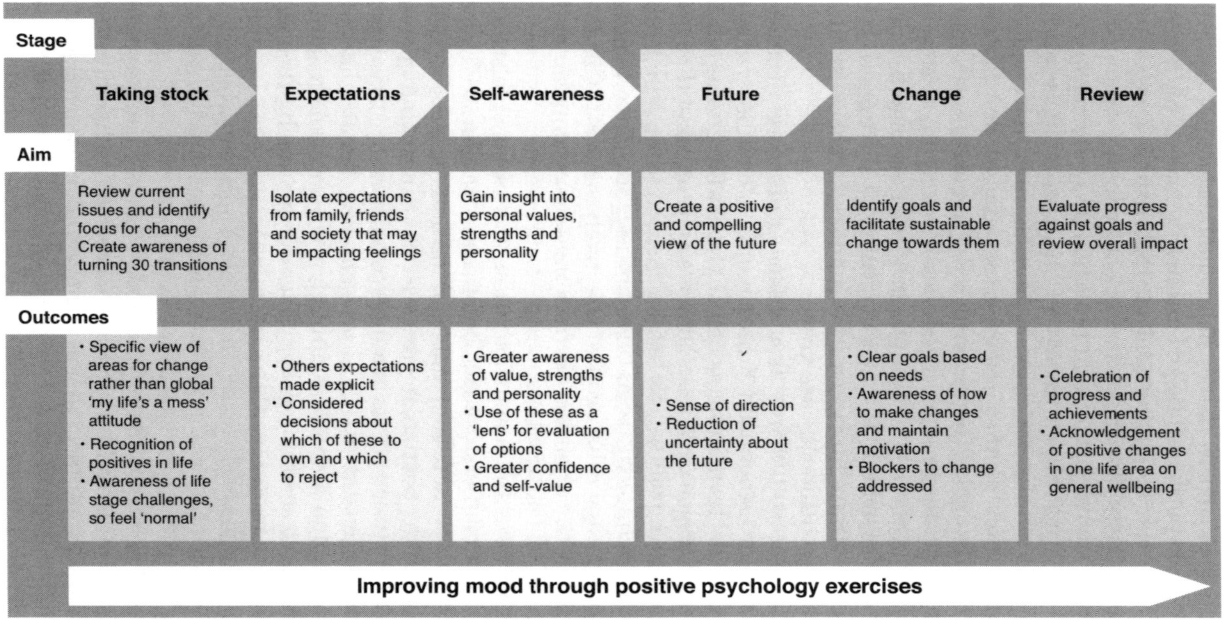

| Stage | Taking stock | Expectations | Self-awareness | Future | Change | Review |
|---|---|---|---|---|---|---|
| **Aim** | Review current issues and identify focus for change. Create awareness of turning 30 transitions | Isolate expectations from family, friends and society that may be impacting feelings | Gain insight into personal values, strengths and personality | Create a positive and compelling view of the future | Identify goals and facilitate sustainable change towards them | Evaluate progress against goals and review overall impact |
| **Outcomes** | • Specific view of areas for change rather than global 'my life's a mess' attitude<br>• Recognition of positives in life<br>• Awareness of life stage challenges, so feel 'normal' | • Others expectations made explicit<br>• Considered decisions about which of these to own and which to reject | • Greater awareness of value, strengths and personality<br>• Use of these as a 'lens' for evaluation of options<br>• Greater confidence and self-value | • Sense of direction<br>• Reduction of uncertainty about the future | • Clear goals based on needs<br>• Awareness of how to make changes and maintain motivation<br>• Blockers to change addressed | • Celebration of progress and achievements<br>• Acknowledgement of positive changes in one life area on general wellbeing |

Improving mood through positive psychology exercises

*Figure 4.2* Coaching model for 'turning 30' transitions

relationships and work–life balance. These skills underpin the optimum performance and ultimate retention of the graduate. They can be encouraged through training, or perhaps more effectively through mentoring or coaching.

Talent development and retention programmes are also of value, with the 'turning 30' transition in mind. By supporting individuals, organisations increase the chance of retaining them as they review their careers and consider other life changes. When joining an organisation, graduates tend to experience structured development for the initial years, but in their late 20s and early 30s they may be left to fend for themselves, just as their value to the organisation increases. Many organisations find that their attrition figures rise within this age group.

'Reverse mentoring' is another useful organisational approach for Generation Y individuals, particularly during the 'early 20s' transition, as one of the challenges here is for people to become organisationally 'savvy' and feel that their skills are being valued. By asking them to tutor senior executives in technology, social networking, etc., they feel that their knowledge is being used effectively, and in the process learn about the organisation from the senior manager whilst building their network.

In terms of the coach, both those at a similar life stage or a more senior life stage can be effective: the former may be perceived to be more empathic, and the latter wiser. An understanding of the particular pressures, challenges and opportunities facing young adults in today's social context is important.

Two case studies will now be covered. The first is based on coaching an individual through a 'turning 30' transition. The second describes a group coaching approach taken with a group of late 20-something top talent.

## Case study 1

The coachee was a 32-year-old male who had been assigned an executive coach by his HR manager. He had been recently promoted to a senior position at work and had moved in with his long-term girlfriend. His primary concern was a lack of confidence in his new role. When questioned further he also stated that he felt 'stressed' and run-down in general, and was finding less time for himself given the recent changes in his life.

The coaching took the format of three face-to-face sessions. During the initial session, the coachee completed an audit of different life areas. His highest scoring areas were finances and relationships. Lowest scores were for health, work and lifestyle. The questions he wanted to focus on during coaching were: 'What do I want from my career?', 'How do I maintain my independence whilst in a relationship?' and 'How do I stay healthy?'.

The coachee completed a visioning exercise 'Letter from the Future' (Grant and Greene, 2004). He described a future life where he felt healthy and energised, relaxed at work, had time for himself and was planning a family with his partner. Another aspect of the coaching encouraged the coachee to consider the external expectations he was living with. This led to insights that his parents, girlfriend and boss expected him to be successful at work and to continue to climb the career ladder, whereas this may not be what he wanted, having already reached a senior position.

Adopting a strengths coaching approach based on positive psychology (e.g. Seligman, 2003), the coachee completed the Values in Action (VIA) strengths survey (Peterson and Seligman, 2004) and the Myers-Briggs Type Indicator (MBTI) personality measure. This led to greater self-awareness and ideas for how to use his strengths most effectively within his new role. Other positive psychology tools included listing 'three good things' on a daily basis and listing career successes to date.

A transition perspective was also discussed as part of the coaching process, in light of the recent changes in his life. He had been in a specialist role for a number of years, with which he was familiar and felt comfortable, and his new role was a significantly more senior position with the associated challenges. In a similar timeframe he had met and moved in with his girlfriend, transitioning quickly from an independent bachelor lifestyle to co-habitation. The coachee found it useful to explore some of the emotions associated with these transitions (e.g. Bridges, 1995), and to acknowledge these as normal responses to change.

As a result of the coaching process, the coachee set achievable health and exercise goals, such as committing to play squash on a weekly basis. He also decided to set limits on the time he was spending at work, in order to have a better work–life balance. He acknowledged that the transition from an independent lifestyle to co-habitation was challenging, yet was taking him towards the future he wanted. He realised he did not need to give all his non-work time to his relationship and that some independent time was necessary and healthy.

The realisation that the expectations of continued career acceleration were external released some of the pressure he was experiencing with regard to his new role. Greater awareness of his strengths and career successes boosted his confidence and led to practical strategies to move forward with.

This coaching case study provides a good illustration of an individual dealing with the demands of the 'turning 30' transition. One of the key challenges he was facing was balancing intimacy with independence, as per Erikson's (1950) theory. He was transitioning from one life structure to another (Levinson, 1986), and coaching provided a space to consider these changes and enhance self-awareness in order to move forward in a positive manner. Coaching, positive, developmental and generational psychology offered useful perspectives and tools to support this individual.

## Case study 2

The organisational case study concerns a group coaching programme for a number of high-potential late 20-somethings. The aim of the programme was to reward, develop and retain junior talent. It was designed to provide individuals with the self-awareness required to make informed and sustainable life and career decisions. A number of skills for success were covered: work–life balance, negotiating life transitions and managing pressure.

The programme took the format of three 1-day coaching workshops, with an informal and creative style. It was introduced by the senior sponsor and positioned as a confidential personal development experience, which reflected how much the participants were valued by the organisation as emerging leaders. Participants were introduced to the concept of life transitions, in terms of the psychological processes and the generational influences and expectations relevant to them. Individuals were encouraged to take stock of their lives and imagine the future. A number of exercises focused on increasing self-awareness, including the VIA survey and MBTI. Pressure management and work–life balance strategies were covered, which incorporated cognitive-behavioural components as well as relaxation techniques. To complete the programme, participants considered questions of happiness, purpose and meaning. They were encouraged to complete a number of exercises deriving from the positive psychology literature (e.g. Seligman, 2003), such as writing a gratitude letter to someone they wanted to express thanks to. Finally, each participant presented their learning to the group in an individual way. They left with a sense of their purpose and meaning in life, greater self-insight and some goals for the future. Review comments include:

*'I have a great deal in life to be grateful for.'*

*'Life isn't all about work. If I make better use of my time outside of work, my career will also benefit.'*

*'I feel more positive, confident and ready to tackle challenges.'*

Several months later, the senior sponsor arranged a dinner for the group so that they could reflect on the programme and share their insights. He spoke about his own experiences of his 30s and how greater self-insight would have enabled him to make better life and career decisions. He shared the fact that he wanted to give the group the knowledge and insight they would need to negotiate their 'turning 30' transitions in a positive and informed way.

## Discussion issues

1   What impact does the increased use of technology have on the challenges and opportunities faced by today's 20- and 30-somethings?

2 Is increased choice a positive or negative social change?
3 Is 'career for life' an outdated concept?
4 How does the 'cult of celebrity' contribute to the experience of early adulthood?

## Endnote

1 Quotes are qualitative data from questionnaires or coaching clients (see Panchal and Jackson, 2007: 47).

## References

Arnett, J. J. (2000) Emerging adulthood: A theory of development from the late teens through the twenties. *American Psychologist*, *55*: 469–480.

Barr, D. (2004) *Get It Together: A Guide to Surviving Your Quarterlife Crisis*. London: Hodder & Stoughton.

Bridges, W. (1995) *Managing Transitions: Making the Most of Change*. London: Nicholas Brealey.

CIPD (Chartered Institute of Personnel and Development) (2008) *Gen Up: How the Four Generations Work*. London: CIPD. Retrieved from http://www.cipd.co.uk/onlineinfodocuments on 15 March 2009.

Common Purpose (2004) *Searching for Something: Exploring the Career Traps and Ambitions of Young People*. London: Common Purpose. Retrieved from http://www.commonpurpose.org.uk/media/36828/searching_for_something.pdf on 6 January 2010.

Coupland, D. (1991) *Generation X: Tales for an Accelerated Culture*. New York: St Martin's Griffin.

Dunn, T. R. and Merriam, S. B. (1995) Levinson's age-thirty transition: Does it exist? *Journal of Adult Development*, *2*: 113–124.

Eisner, S. P. (2005) Managing Generation Y. *SAM Advanced Management Journal*, *70*: 4–13.

Erikson, E. (1950) *Childhood and Society*. New York: Norton.

Fox, K. (2005) *Coming of Age in the eBay Generation: Life-Shopping and the New Life Skills in the Age of eBay*. Oxford: Social Issues Research Centre. Retrieved from http://www.sirc.org/publik/Yeppies.pdf on 20 October 2008.

Furnham, A. (2008, November) *The Psychology of Money*. Invited address to BPS London and Home Counties Branch, London.

Gergen, K. J. (1991) *The Saturated Self*. New York: Basic Books.

Gould, R. (1978) *Transformations*. New York: Simon & Schuster.

Grant, A. and Greene, J. (2004) *Coach Yourself: It's Your Life, What Are You Going To Do With It?* London: Pearson Education.

Holmes, T. H. and Rahe, R. H. (1967) Social readjustment rating scale. *Journal of Psychosomatic Research*, *11*: 213–218.

Levinson, D. J. (1986) A conception of adult development. *American Psychologist*, *41*: 3–13.

Levinson, D. J. (1996) *The Seasons of a Woman's Life*. New York: Random House.

Office for National Statistics (2009a, February) *News Release – Marriage Rates Fall to Lowest on Record*. Retrieved from http://www.statistics.gov.uk/pdfdir/marr0209.pdf on 12 September 2009.

Office for National Statistics (2009b, May) *Statistical Bulletin*. Retrieved from http://www.statistics.gov.uk/pdfdir/bdths0509.pdf on 11 January 2010.

Panchal, S. and Jackson, E. (2005) *Turning 30: How to Get the Life You Really Want*. London: Piatkus Books.

Panchal, S. and Jackson, E. (2007). 'Turning 30' transitions: Generation Y hits quarter-life. *Coaching Psychologist*, *3*: 46–51.

Peterson, C. and Seligman, M. (2004). *Character Strengths and Virtues: A Handbook and Classification*. New York: American Psychological Association and Oxford University Press.

Pew Research Center (2007) *How Young People View Their Lives, Futures and Politics: A Portrait of Generation Next*. Survey conducted in association with the Generation Next Initiative and documentary produced by MacNeil/Lehrer Productions.

Push Student Debt Survey (2009) Retrieved from http://news.sky.com/skynews/Home/Business/Student-Debt-Average-Graduate-Will-Owe-23500-On-Leaving-University-Says-PushSurvey/Article/200908315363722?f=rss on 12 October 2009.

Redmond, P. (2009, February) *Generation Y: Maximising the Value of Generations in the 21st Century Workplace*. Presentation for Government Legal Service.

Reinke, B. J., Holmes, D. S. and Harris, R. L. (1985) The timing of psychosocial changes in women's lives: The years 25 to 45. *Journal of Personality and Social Psychology*, *48*: 1353–1364.

Robbins, A. and Wilner, A. (2001) *Quarterlife Crisis: The Unique Challenges of Life in Your Twenties*. New York: Tarcher.

Roisman, G. I., Masten, A. S., Coatsworth, J. D. and Tellegen, A. (2004) Salient and emerging developmental tasks in the transition to adulthood. *Child Development*, *75*: 123–133.

Schwartz, B. (2003) *The Paradox of Choice: Why More is Less*. New York: Ecco.

Seligman, M (2003) *Authentic Happiness*. London: Nicholas Brealey.

Sheehy, G. (1976) *Passages: Predictable Crises of Adult Life*. New York: Dutton.

Sheehy, G. (1995) *New Passages: Mapping your Life Across Time*. London: Random House.

## Recommended reading

Panchal, S. and Jackson, E. (2005) *Turning 30: How To Get The Life You Really Want*. London: Piatkus Books.

Robbins, A. and Wilner, A. (2001) *Quarterlife Crisis: The Unique Challenges of Life in Your Twenties*. New York: Tarcher.

# 5

# Becoming a parent

## *Jennifer Liston-Smith*

'Do you want to have kids when you grow up?' Becoming a parent marks a uniquely *optional* transition that is possible over a large age range. We assume we have a choice but sometimes the opposite happens. Either way, the result is profoundly transformative in practical and emotional ways affecting identity, career, social life, relationships, finances and well-being for women and for men.

Becoming a parent brings primary and lasting responsibility for a baby or child (several in multiple births). In practice, it may be transient – a woman giving birth to a stillborn baby takes 'maternity' leave under UK and similar legislation. The teenager with a substance dependency who 'gives' her newborn baby up for adoption yet cries on his birthday each year arguably has also transitioned to parenthood. For most, parenthood is ongoing and presents fresh challenges at each phase.

Parenting has diverse models: single people, mixed-sex couples, same-sex couples, families in polygamous cultures, people who adopt from within their own culture or from far outside, those who foster children for a time and stepfamilies. Today it can involve: groups of people in collaborative procreation through surrogacy; those whose conception, pregnancy or birth is enabled or assisted by technology or bioscience; those in poverty or otherwise who are disadvantaged for lack of these; or those shunning intervention and aiming to be personally empowered by taking a natural approach.

The transition to parenthood spans a broader sliding scale of ages than most transitions featured in this book. A particularly wide range is possible for men, including second or third families, with serial or parallel partners. Today, Generation Y individuals become parents alongside Baby Boomers, with some of those older parents choosing in vitro fertilisation when 'nature' would otherwise have closed down the window of opportunity.

In stepfamilies, children can find they have nieces and nephews older than themselves, through half-brothers or -sisters, and a man or woman may become a grandparent in the same year as they become, again, a parent to a younger child with their original or new partner.

Between 2001 and 2008, the average age of childbearing and the overall number of live births increased year on year in England and Wales: 708,708 babies were born in the region in 2008 and the mean age of women giving birth was 29.3 years. The number of live births to mothers aged 40 years and over nearly doubled from 13,555 in 1998 to 26,419 in 2008 (Office for National Statistics, 2009).

## Cultural and societal context

Becoming a parent has commonality across cultures in its biological and main practical implications yet may be interpreted and experienced differently. Intergenerational factors may be especially strong in some cultures through the influence (welcomed or otherwise) of grandparents and wider or extended family. In cultures where families have tended to live in isolated nuclear units, and the cost of living and other trends lead increasingly to dual-career families, grandparents may play a greater role in childcare while mothers work.

Generational changes have affected the cultural context of fatherhood. There is a greater focus on nurturing as well as breadwinning, which has clear upsides but may introduce the stress of role ambiguity and conflict. This could be an issue for both parents, as conventional couples move away from the clarity of defined and separate roles.

With technological advancement, the window of opportunity for motherhood is ever-extending. Still, some high-flying women, focused on a career in a world of work still arguably built on a male model of long hours and single-minded dedication, are suddenly shocked to find they have left it too late to really 'have it all'. And in a world of feminism, post-feminism and backlash, today's women may question the pursuit of the 'superwoman'. Certainly, the media continue to host fierce debate about the value of all these stances, which perhaps adds to the burden of the transition as women may feel criticised for their choices. Arguably, though, in these times of constant re-thinking and deconstructing, any one choice is as valid as any other. That said, missing out on parenting without intending to can be experienced with a painful sense of loss and grieving at a personal level.

Those who opt, without deep regret, to continue as non-parents may at some point experience that decision 'not to' as a transition in their lives – a choice to be celebrated or even relished as they watch their peers juggle, negotiate and dart about in the family 'taxi'.

## Developmental potential

There are many stakeholders in the success of this transition. It can be asserted that parenting offers extraordinary self-development potential for the parent him- or herself. For example, Baby Boomer fathers being coached around retirement wistfully remark that they wish they had spent more time with their families (rather than the office), suggesting after all that it is having children that has given their lives perspective, real meaning and a true sense of legacy.

For both parents, and for every generation, the individual's whole 'place' in the world seems to change overnight on becoming a parent, sometimes bringing a positive sense of being 'finally grown up' and moving up in the 'family hierarchy'.

In popular myth, women become expert multi-taskers and mediators as mums, and many who comfortably adjust to parenthood also become more assertive on behalf of their family's needs in the world, whilst also being more community-aware and attuned to sustainability in terms of their overall world view. Some feel that by getting a taste for what we can call unconditional love they are at last more fully themselves and this feeds their spiritual growth. In the sections following, we explore some elements of this personal development more closely.

## *Parental pressures*

Having a baby has been ranked sixth out of 102 stressful life events (Dohrenwend, Krasnoff and Askenasy, 1978). Cowan and Cowan's (1988) literature review concluded that the transition is equally disruptive for men and women and for a couple, and that, at least in the early period, the changes are more negative than positive.

Brotherson (2004) suggests that the top transition issues for new parents include:

- **For men**
  - Financially providing for the family
  - Lack of sleep and tiredness
  - Increased chores and housework
  - Intrusive in-laws
  - Loss of free time for self and social activities
  - Decline in spouse's sexual interest
  - Couple disagreements about roles.

- **For women**
  - Lack of sleep and tiredness
  - Changes in body figure
  - Personal doubts about parental competence or skills
  - Unpredictable shifts in mood and anxiety
  - Dissatisfaction with personal appearance
  - Increased chores and housework
  - Individual stress about roles and responsibilities
  - Change in work situation.

For new parents in a couple relationship (the norm in Traditionalists, Baby Boomers and, still to a surprising extent, Generation X), Belsky and Kelly (1994) identified five areas of potential disagreement (division of labour, money, work, relationship, social life) and concluded that 'couples who manage to resolve these issues in a mutually satisfying way generally become happier with their marriages, whereas those who do not become unhappier' (1994: 32). Less developed problem-solving abilities and conflict strategies (Cox et al., 1999) and more strain in a marriage (Cowan and Cowan, 1992) before the birth are associated with worse outcomes afterwards.

Wylie (1979) suggests a positive relationship between prenatal expectations and ease of the transition, and according to Pancer and associates (2000) 'increased complexity' in thinking about one's expectations at the transition to parenthood appears to result in 'better adjustment for women after the birth of a child'.

Differing expectations and outcomes between first-time biological and adoptive parents were explored by Levy-Shiff, Goldshmidt and Har-Even (1991). The adoptive parents in their study of 104 couples had more positive expectations and reported more satisfying experiences in their transition to parenthood than did the biological parents. At the same time, results suggested that the processes underlying the transition to parenthood in adoptive and biological families differ. While overall 'the predictors of parental experiences were parental expectations and depressive mood' for both groups, for the biological parents a further predictor was ego strength and for the adoptive parents it was 'feelings of deprivation, social support and self-concept'.

All the specific factors sit within a fundamental shift in the dynamic of the relationship for an existing couple. According to Systems Theory (e.g. P. Minuchin, 1988; S. Minuchin, 1974; von Bertalanffy, 1975), the addition of a baby transforms a dyad (e.g. male–female or same-sex couple) into a triad and therefore adds complexity to the system. For a couple, there are three subsystems – each of the two individuals and the relationship between them. After a baby is born, there are seven subsystems – each individual, three dyadic relationships (e.g. mother and child, mother and father, father and child) and the relationship between all three together. Change in any one area affects the others and also their wider relationships, such as with grandparents and with key individuals or institutions outside the family (e.g. work, friends and childcare providers) (Cowan and Cowan, 1992).

## The upside, developmentally

Despite the potential challenges, parenthood can be embraced as a normal developmental event for an adult or couple (Miller and Sollie, 1980) and as far back as the late 1960s Rossi (1968) exhorted us to view this as a 'transition' rather than a 'crisis'.

Parenting can bring personal fulfillment and de Marneffe (2004) suggests that we reconstruct mothering as 'a positive aspect of the self' and that the emotional journey of motherhood can promote individual growth and development. She writes that maternal desire:

> is not the duty to mother, or the compulsion to mother, or the concession to mothering when other options are not available. . . . It is the longing felt by a mother to nurture her children; the wish to participate in their mutual relationship; and the choice, insofar as it is possible, to put her desire into practice.
>
> (de Marneffe, 2004: 3)

Liston-Smith and Chapman (2009) highlight the developmental power of working motherhood: 'Female leaders are discovering that the "mothering" skills they acquire on maternity leave are also distinctly new talents critical to successful leadership.' When independent researcher Margaret Chapman observed group maternity coaching at a global financial services company (Liston-Smith and Chapman, 2008) she was struck by 'the paradoxical way the women lost confidence in their executive roles while gaining a sense of empowerment in motherhood'. Chapman comments: 'It was striking how the women had acquired a whole set of skills and capabilities that were seemingly out of their awareness yet revealed distinctly new talents critical to successful leadership' (Chapman, 2008).

Should there be limits on our empowerment or enjoyment in motherhood? The Children's Society's report entitled *The Good Childhood Inquiry* concluded:

Most of the obstacles children face today are linked to the belief among adults that the prime duty of the individual is to make the most of their own life, rather than contribute to the good of others. . . . excessive individualism is causing a range of problems for children including: high family break-up, teenage unkindness, commercial pressures towards premature sexualisation, unprincipled advertising, too much competition in education and acceptance of income inequality.

(The Children's Society, 2009)

The controversial report (Layard and Dunn, 2009: 6) suggests that 'although freedom and self-determination bring many blessings, the balance has tilted too far towards individualism in Britain'.

### *Specific motherhood themes*

My busy working life was replaced by long days that seemed to pass in slow motion, trapped in the world of the baby . . . For many women this is intolerable. For others, it is a pleasantly dreamy world . . . freed from the burdens of being a striving, achieving self. But probably for most women who have a sense of identity based on their working lives, it is a very difficult adjustment.

(Gerhardt, 2004: 208)

Daniel Stern (1995) pinpoints four major themes arising during pregnancy that continue for the first 12–18 months of a child's life:

- **Life growth**. Will I survive? Can I keep my baby alive? Is the baby still breathing? Is the baby getting enough milk?
- **Primary relatedness**. Can I love my baby? How will I know my baby loves me? Am I a 'natural' mother?
- **Supporting matrix**. Who will value, appreciate and support me (at home and work)? Who cares and understands my situation? Will the independent career-minded woman recognise the need for support or accept emotional or practical support?

- **Identity reorganisation**. Who am I? What's important
  in life? Motherhood or career or both?

These themes are set in a context in which – during pregnancy – many women become more interested in goals related
to motherhood ('to be a good mother') and less interested in
achievement-related goals ('to make career decisions')
(Salmela-Aro et al., 2000).

Smith's (1999) qualitative research describes a complex
journey in which there is not so much a shift from outer
world to inner world during middle pregnancy (e.g. Gloger-
Tippelt, 1983; Shereshefsky and Yarrow, 1973), but a shift
to a kind of exquisite balance between the two as well
as a situation in which the outer world is increasingly
more about family and friends than about the world of
work.

Millward (2006) further explores the subtle dance of
redefining identity while also being treated differently by
others. Here the chief impact of the transition appeared in
the women's changed sense of identity and in their experience of the 'psychological contract' with their employers.
Women, in professional or managerial jobs, reportedly felt
'progressively disengaged from their jobs and their organization' from the moment of announcing their pregnancy.

Sometimes, transition themes merge into mental health
issues. For many women, a few days or weeks of feeling down,
adjusting, getting over the birth is a familiar part of the
Baby Blues. Up to 12–13% experience depression either peri-
natally (during pregnancy) or postnatally (up to 6 months
after delivery) (Hendrick, 2003).

## *Fatherhood themes*

Increasingly, men are more involved in child-rearing as well
as birth. Parr (1996) indicated that men are concerned not
only about their baby's survival and growth but also that of
their wife/partner. Where a relationship breaks up, Florsheim
and associates (2003) found that the quality of the pre-birth
partner relationship buffered the impact of this on a young
father's adjustment to parenthood.

As Stern (1995) found of mothers, fathers demonstrate some concern about 'primary relatedness' with the baby and their own 'identity reorganisation'.

In-depth research by Crabb and Millward (2008) found that men position themselves between the dual pulls of child and breadwinning work (Crabb, 2008). Seward and Richter (2008: 89) speak of the negotiation that must take place when roles are no longer defined and fixed in society:

> Whether a father takes parental leave or how much he shares household chores are more than just matters of economic and legal prescriptions. . . . In advanced societies, behavior in family positions is not self evident. According to the theory of individualization, negotiations in society occur on many different levels. Negotiations during interactions occur between intimate partners on a micro level . . . On a macro level, the negotiations occur between competing agencies and institutions . . . especially as they relate to the challenges of combining family and work.

Will dads now repeat the whole journey that mothers have unfolded before them, wrestling with the barriers – such as lack of quality part-time work – that interfere with combining career and parenthood?

## The missed transition

It is not only giving birth that can surface painful emotions and confusion. The ground-breaking work of Hewlett (2002) revealed the difficulty that the Baby Boomer generation had lived with in striving to combine career and family and the sense of loss for many on discovering they had left it too late:

> There is a secret out there – a painful, well-kept secret: At midlife, between a third and a half of all successful career women in the United States do not have children. . . . . These women have not chosen to remain childless. The vast majority, in fact, yearn for children. Indeed, some have gone to extraordinary lengths to bring a baby into their lives. . . . In the words of one senior manager,

the typical high-achieving woman childless at midlife
had not made a choice but a 'creeping nonchoice'.

(Hewlett, 2002: 4)

The depth of feeling associated with infertility and
reproductive decisions for both women and men is touchingly
captured by Pawson (2003). Speaking separately on this theme
at a conference entitled '*Challenging the "good" death*', Pawson
insists:

There are three absolute 'givens' in our existence:- death
is inevitable, we are spiritually alone in this world; there
is no known purpose to life. Having a child does alleviate
the stark awfulness of these existential problems. By
having a child and passing on genes you are getting as
close as you can to immortality.

(Pawson, quoted in Liston-Smith, 2002: 15)

### *Generational factors*

Traditionalists and then Baby Boomers took their turns in
hand-crafting and then mass-producing the less-defined gender
roles we live today. For Generation X, the stakes are high and
parenthood is a shock in the way it messes with identity.

But what will Generation Y make of all this angst and
proving of oneself? Can we actually have it all and is that
even the point? Douglas and Michaels (2004) argue that the
media cult of blissed-out celebrity mums set back the femi-
nist agenda. Nonetheless the savvy new self-realisers and
blogging mumpreneurs will make their own rules, whether
supermum, career woman or surrendered to de Marneffe's
(2004) maternal desire (see above).

Generation Y are growing up in a world with rapidly
changing expectations about work and life. The 2006
*Investigation into the Transformation of Work* by the former
Equal Opportunities Commission (EOC, 2007) revealed that
half the workforce wanted to work more flexible hours (52%
of men and 48% of women). The report also predicted that by
2010 less than 20% of the workforce would be made up of
white, non-disabled men under 45 in full-time work. Forward-
thinking organisations would look at flexibility in a different

way, in order to attract diverse, talented people looking for a new relationship with work, combining successful careers with caring and lifestyle choices. So, Generation Y might embrace parenthood while forging leadership roles built on its developmental foundation, or simply relish the personal growth and fulfillment in being a parent in and of itself.

Generation Y are much more at home with all forms of diversity – gender, ethnic and otherwise. Paradoxically, this might enable a positive gathering up of more deeply traditional ways, woven into a multi-cultural lifestyle. A factsheet entitled *Understanding Postnatal Depression* published by MIND suggests:

> Rituals help us to adjust. An Indian health-worker, now living in the UK, put it as follows, 'During our visit home to Gujerat, my sister-in-law gave birth. She did no housework for 40 days, just lay in bed with the baby, and we, the women of the family, all sat around bringing her presents, singing and gossiping and telling stories. Every day, the midwife came and gave her and the baby a massage'.
>
> (Cloutte and Darton, 2008: 8)

## Coach or mentor?

A parent coach is not there to pass on their own experience in 'if I were you' or 'well, this sorted mine out' mode. An element of mentoring arises from a new mother's need for a mother-figure at this time (Stern, 1995), and having gone through the transition oneself is a good foundation for genuine empathy.

There is a delicate dynamic, then. A coachee never signs up for 'tips and hints' if they really embrace coaching; however, they are often desperate to ask the parent coach 'but what did *you* do?'. The mentor-coach in this situation holds her (or his) experience as developmental; not as the blueprint for the success of the coachee. There is a valuable sense of 'having been there'; yet, perhaps more than in most coaching situations, the mentor-coach wrestles with a huge urge to give advice, knowing that truly empowering coaching enables the person to find their own solutions.

The power of the coach simply being with the new parent, allowing him or her to find their own voice, is underlined in Smith's (1999) work. Participants commented that taking part in the research and exploring the transition to motherhood without being judged had been a beneficial experience, helping them 'get things off my chest' and having the option to 'modify how I operate' (Smith, 1999: 297).

## *Client groups and contexts*

Who asks for coaching at this transition? Clients may be self-funding, although since 2005 'maternity coaching' has become established as an intervention bought in by Human Resources and Diversity Specialists in organisations (e.g. Clarke, 2007; Lucas, 2008).

Coachees may include the following:

- Women in professional or managerial roles, privately funded or supported by an employer. Established in their careers, some would perceive that these clients have 'a lot to lose' as they enter motherhood.
- Men, and women, who may bring new parenthood responsibilities to wider coaching as a new context that challenges established patterns.
- Staff in organisations that offer maternity/parent coaching as an investment across their whole employee group through policies of being family-friendly and retaining talented and diverse employees.
- Parents identified as benefiting from particular support through reasons of social exclusion or being very young parents, especially teenagers, accessing coaching-based parenting programmes provided via Children's Centres and similar Sure Start type programmes, often with public funding.
- Women contemplating entrepreneurship at this transition, viewing business ownership as a means of having more control over work–life balance.
- Successful applicants for employer-hosted programmes encouraging women (and men) back to work after a career break associated with parenting (e.g. Kinsey, 2008).

## *Main themes of parent transition coaching*

Overall the coaching holds an awareness of the research-based themes of transition, while mindful of the context and purpose within which it is taking place. The understanding of a 'successful' transition needs to be clarified with the relevant stakeholders at the outset.

During maternity coaching, there is a dual focus on the personal and professional/work-related. At the level of the self, the individual is coming to terms with the losses and gains of the new role, taking stock of the paradox of personal growth in her new life phase alongside the huge challenges and limitations given her new responsibility. Often there is an unaccustomed urgency to state her own needs and accept practical help. Professionally, the themes are about having more strategic influence and visibility while finding increasingly smart ways of building work–life balance.

Paternity coaching reflects some similar themes to maternity as well as exploring any role conflict between a stronger drive to perform as 'breadwinner' alongside a pull towards a caring role as involved parent and supportive partner. Like mothers, a new father may feel an unexpected cocktail of positive and negative emotions.

## Core coaching approaches and techniques with new parents

Given the delicate state of self-identity at the transition, a person-centred foundation is important, accepting the new or expectant parent as and where they are and drawing out an agenda and action plan with their concerns and goals at the heart.

## *Setting the agenda*

The agenda should be renegotiated at different phases, for example:

1 During pregnancy (before maternity leave).
2 After giving birth while still on maternity leave.
3 Following return to work.

This 'revisiting' approach provides continuity and prompting at a time when it may be hard truly to remember what one's priorities and aspirations were at an earlier stage.

Where an employer is funding the coaching, the use of a central (confidential) self-assessment based on core areas relevant to the transition (e.g. Liston-Smith, 2009) gives consistency to the intervention. It addresses the employer's expectation that the coaching will explore a broad context of work and life, while essentially personalised and practically relevant.

## *Positive psychology*

Positive psychology interventions are highly relevant in coaching new parents. Confidence may be enhanced through coaching for strengths (Linley et al., 2006; Seligman and Peterson, 2004) rather than focusing on deficits in the parenting role, especially since individuals applying their strengths in a new way can expect increased happiness and decreased depressive symptoms for 6 months (Seligman et al., 2005). Similarly relevant to parenting is the exercise of identifying, daily, 'three good things' that have occurred, as in the case study below.

## *Cognitive-behavioural coaching*

Cognitive-behavioural coaching (e.g. Palmer and Szymanska, 2007) has been offered to new parents in settings from global law and finance firms to Sure Start programmes (Liston-Smith, 2006).

High-achieving women (and men) can struggle with perfectionism on return to work and the organisational culture may confirm to them that others are just waiting for them to trip up. Instead of spotting how they fall short of high standards as working parents, they can explore how to stay goal-focused and productive by challenging negative assumptions. The ultimate aim is to be strategic rather than reactive (Liston-Smith, 2005).

## *Compassionate or non-violent communication*

In a context of societal and generational change, the new parent needs to articulate their own needs and be flexible and attentive in understanding the needs of others. Old assumptions (prejudices perhaps) no longer hold up.

Rosenberg's (2003) non-violent communication framework, identifying observations, feelings, needs and requests, helps the new parent ask for support while avoiding phrasing it as a demand or a generalised judgement ('You never help around the house'), which leads the listener to defend themselves instead of hearing or being able to help.

## Environment and logistics

One-to-one parent coaching provides a confidential space to process emotions, plans and new perspectives. Group coaching can open up transformative conversations that simply do not otherwise take place at work, leading to shared resources and a sense of normalisation and possibility. One group participant puts it: 'being together, part of a group; it gives a sense of power, knowing that all working mothers struggle – maybe we maintain a face at work but being in the group together brings perspective' (Liston-Smith and Chapman, 2008).

Coaching for parents in transition has been found to be effective (the coachee reports that it met their agreed needs and organisation-level satisfaction) whether undertaken in protected space in the workplace, off-site in training premises, in the coachee's own home, by individual telephone coaching call or by group teleconference. Internal coach teams within organisations can be supported with understanding of the transition and tools to enhance their coaching for this group.

e-Coaching, text coaching and social/professional online networks have a valuable place in this transition, particularly during maternity leave, including accessing support networks based in the workplace. This can be particularly useful for Generation Y mothers, who tend to use online tools such as Facebook for informal mutual coaching,

## Supervision, feedback and referring on

With parenthood coaching, supervision plays an important role in enhancing professional development as well as client safety. A supervisor may bring knowledge of perinatal depression, specialist understanding of early parenting experiences, a developmental interest in the parenting transition and organisational experience where the coaching takes place in a corporate context.

Where the coaching is employer-sponsored, an organisational feedback process can be beneficial: participants' experiences enrich and inform the employer's maternity, paternity and adoption policies and practices through a confidential channel. This is in addition to the usual end-of-intervention evaluation by the coachee against her coaching objectives.

The parent coach's checklist for onward referral includes awareness of the indicators of perinatal depression, which, for example, would likely benefit from specific cognitive-behavioural therapy (NICE, 2007). One particularly helpful workplace referral point is an Employee Assistance Programme (EAP). Good EAPs provide counselling support and also practical advice such as childcare provision and knowing one's rights as an expectant or new parent. Having access to such a service helps the parent transition coach focus on coaching rather than simply signposting information.

## Case study

Rachel is a middle manager in a large business services firm. Regarded as ambitious, talented, self-motivating and proactive, Rachel was shocked at her loss of confidence as her return to work approached.

Rachel completed the Maternity Project™ Questionnaire (see Liston-Smith, 2009) before maternity leave, revealing both optimism and anxiety and a huge to-do list preparing for her leave. She was keen to pick up where she left off after maternity leave, and her goal was to protect her career prospects in terms of seniority and reputation while reducing her hours (and pay) to 4 days a week and also enjoying motherhood. She was concerned she would lose touch with some major organisational changes while away and admitted to feeling 'threatened' as she worried her team members would prefer the person covering her role in her absence.

*The coaching*

Rachel's employer sponsored:

- a 2-hour face-to-face coaching session off-site before maternity or adoption leave;
- two 60-minute phone coaching calls during maternity leave;
- a further 60-minute coaching call a month after return.

A coaching contract established boundaries, number and format of sessions and expectations regarding contact, such as email follow-up. There was a clear understanding that coaching was provided by the employer with the aim of supporting and also retaining employees through this transition for a confident, effective return.

Rachel's first session identified opportunities and strategies for an effective, influential handover and options for staying in contact during maternity leave, including working occasional Keeping in Touch days prior to her return. She also clarified some points for her flexible working application, making a business case for her revised hours in terms of her enhanced loyalty and productivity if she could work her chosen pattern. This helped her feel more 'in control' at a time when everything seemed to be in question. She took away reading material on the research-based themes of the transition, although at this point she thought the suggestion of new needs for support including other mothers was 'not really me'.

By the second session, 4 months after giving birth, Rachel was reeling with a sense of 'not getting anything done'.

*Rachel:*    Saul is active and lively and it's just the best thing being his mother. But I feel a bit of a failure in terms of my coaching goals. The problem is, I spend ages sitting around with him, meeting all his needs in a fairly low key way and things drift into my mind then about contacting my manager or team and networking and all that. Next thing is, I hardly have time to go to the loo or drink a whole cup of tea, let alone being a strategic career woman!

*Coach:*   I'm glad to hear you and Saul are getting along well! It sounds as though there's quite a tension for you between the slow pace of meeting his needs and the flurry of tasks that enter your mind when you stop to think. I'm wondering whether you've noticed in amongst that all the bits of motherhood that you're actually doing well or even just OK?

*Rachel:*   Well, it's mostly pretty straightforward stuff!

*Coach:*   What sort of things?

*Rachel:*   Well, um, bathing him, changing his nappy – he likes me singing to him then – getting out for some fresh air every day, going to this cute baby music class we've just started and I even get organised enough to buy food and cook dinner some days!

*Coach:*   Sounds quite a lot to me. Does it go any way toward offsetting your sense of failure when you list it like that?

*Rachel:*   Well it's my coaching goals I'm failing at but yes, I see what you mean; I'm doing pretty well with Saul, aren't I?

*Coach:*   And . . .?

*Rachel:*   Well it's not all that surprising I haven't been writing daily reports for my boss. I suppose it's early days as well isn't it? I did phone my manager anyway and I've been in to show Saul to the team.

*Coach:*   Does that line up with your goals?

*Rachel:*   Actually, yes. Why didn't I see that: hormone brain or what?

*Coach:*   Well-balanced brain it sounds like to me. How could you make sure you keep sight of these things that go well each day, instead of latching on to the things you've missed?

*Rachel:*   Well I'm not going to keep a spreadsheet of them! *(laughs)*

*Coach:*   How about picturing the good moments in your mind, maybe three of them each day, as you drop off to sleep, or chatting them through with your husband Josh and working out together why they turned out well?

*Rachel:*  I'll treasure them myself I think; yes, I can do that at night, it'll be nice. Actually, that reminds me; you know that idea of needing other women who've been through motherhood as part of your support network: I get it now. My husband just tells me not to be so hard on myself but other mums do really get it: how you can be this high-achieving professional and yet you suddenly feel as though you're starting all over again and you have to rebuild your identity.

*Coach:*  So, tell me a bit more about that, about how it feels to you being a mother and how it's changed you . . .

This dialogue shows a gentle cognitive-behavioural approach to challenging Rachel's 'failure' beliefs by identifying evidence to the contrary and thinking in increments instead of absolutes, followed through with the positive psychology exercise of encouraging her to identify 'three good things' and their causes. This, together with acknowledging Rachel's transition themes, was both pivotal and sufficient at this stage. By session three, just prior to her return, Rachel was ready to draw up some plans – and rehearse conversations – for an assertive approach to leaving work on time while flagging up her successes to maintain her profile.

At her final session, Rachel added that being kinder to herself and counting the 'plus points' in situations also helped her manage the guilt around leaving work on time, as well as the guilt at leaving Saul during the day. We also talked then about her husband Josh and how they could find ways to share with each other more frankly what their support needs now are. eMail was used to send information on non-violent communication as a tool for this and also to elicit anonymous organisational feedback after the close of coaching.

## Discussion issues

1  Is the transition to parenthood more gender-specific than other transitions explored in this book?

2   Who benefits from parent transition coaching? Is it all about the individual parent, or does it promise benefits for the baby/child? Does it provide benefits or challenges for the baby's other parent, where present? Does the 'nanny state' enter into it? Is parent coaching particularly prone to the urge in coaches to give advice, tips and hints when the new mum or dad asks 'but how did you get yours to sleep at night?'?

3   '. . . Now, of course, I realized something else no one tells you; that a child is a grenade. When you have a baby, you set off an explosion in your marriage, and when the dust settles, your marriage is different from what it was. Not better, necessarily; not worse, necessarily; but different' (Ephron, 1983: 158).

    Is having a baby good or bad for a couple relationship?

4   Can a person feel and be fully 'grown up' without going through the huge (but uniquely optional) transition of becoming a parent? Or when we give in to the urge to have children, is it actually 'Game Over' in terms of our own personal adventures?

## References

Belsky, J. and Kelly, J. (1994) *The Transition to Parenthood*. New York: Delacorte Press.

Brotherson, S. (2004, October) *The Transition from Partners to Parents: Bright Beginnings #2*. Fargo, ND: North Dakota State University Extension Service, FS-604.

Chapman, M. A. (2008, February) A preliminary report of a qualitative study into the ICAS/Managing Maternity 'Maternity Matters' Group Coaching Programme (unpublished).

Clarke, A, (2007) Coaching mums – hanging on to talent. *IDS Diversity at Work*, *39*: 11–17.

Cloutte, P. and Darton, K. (2008) *Understanding Postnatal Depression*. Information leaflet. London: MIND.

Cowan, C. P. and Cowan, P. A. (1992) *When Parents Become Partners: The Big Life Change For Couples*. New York: Basic Books.

Cowan, P. A. and Cowan, C. P. (1988) Changes in marriage during the transition to parenthood: Must we blame the baby? In G. Y. Michaels and W. A. Goldberg (Eds.), *The Transition to Parenthood: Current Theory and Research* (pp. 114–154). New York: Cambridge University Press.

Cox, M., Paley, B., Burchinal, M. and Payne, C. (1999) Marital perceptions and interactions across the transition to parenthood. *Journal of Marriage and the Family*, 6: 611–625.

Crabb, S. (2008, Spring) Fathers' experiences of paternity in an organisational context: Q&A discussion with Anna Hayward, Director of Managing Maternity. *Managing Maternity Newsletter 'Maternity Matters'*.

Crabb, S. and Millward, L. J. (2008, January) *Fathers' Experiences of Paternity in an Organizational Context*. Paper presented at the British Psychological Society Division of Occupational Psychology Annual Conference, Stratford-Upon-Avon, UK.

de Marneffe, D. (2004) *Maternal Desire: On Children, Love, and The Inner Life*. New York: Little, Brown & Co.

Dohrenwend, B., Krasnoff, L. and Askenasy, A. (1978) Exemplification of a method for scaling life events. *Journal of Health and Social Behavior*, 19: 205–229.

Douglas, S. and Michaels, M. (2004) *The Mommy Myth: The Mass Media and the Rise of the New Momism*. New York: Free Press.

EOC (Equal Opportunities Commission) (2007) *Enter the Timelords: Final Report of the EOC's Investigation into the Transformation of Work*. London: EOC.

Ephron, N. (1983) *Heartburn*. New York: Knopf.

Florsheim, P., Sumida, E., McCann, C., Winstanley, M., Fukui, R., Seefeldt, T., et al. (2003) The transition to parenthood among young African American and Latino couples: Relational predictors of risk for parental dysfunction. *Journal of Family Psychology*, 1: 65–79.

Gerhardt, S. (2004) *Why Love Matters: How Affection Shapes a Baby's Brain*. Hove, UK: Routledge.

Gloger-Tippelt, G. (1983) A process model of the pregnancy course. *Human Development*, 26: 134–148.

Hendrick, V. (2003) Editorial: Treatment of postnatal depression. *British Medical Journal*, 327:1003–1004.

Hewlett, S. A. (2002) Executive women and the myth of having it all. In S. A. Hewlett, C. Buck Luce and A. Fels (Eds.), *Required Reading for Executive Women – and the Companies Who Need Them*. Boston, MA: Harvard Business School Publishing Corporation. www.hbr.org

Kinsey, J. (2008, March) *Back to IT*. Conference presentation by ThoughtWorks. Presentation at Move out of the Shadow! Seize the OpportunITy, The European Commission Shadowing 2007 Conference, Brussels. Retrieved from http://ec.europa.eu/information_society/activities/itgirls/doc/presentations/workshop_1/thoughtworks_back.ppt on 6 January 2009.

Layard, R. and Dunn, J. (2009) *A Good Childhood: Searching for Values in a Competitive Age*. London: Penguin.

Levy-Shiff, R., Goldshmidt, I. and Har-Even, D. (1991) Transition to parenthood in adoptive families. *Developmental Psychology, 27*: 131–140.

Linley, P. A., Joseph, S., Harrington, S. and Wood, A. M. (2006) Positive psychology: Past, present, and (possible) future. *Journal of Positive Psychology, 1*: 3–16.

Liston-Smith (2002) Conference Report: First National Conference of the Institute of Health Promotion and Education: Challenging the 'good' death: Exploring healthy dying – implications for health promotion and palliative care. *Stress News, 14*: 27–28.

Liston-Smith, J. (2005) Cognitive behavioural coaching with parents. *Stress News, 17*: 5–6.

Liston-Smith, J. (2006, March) Perfectionist Baby Blues – why ambitious high-achieving women may be hit harder by the loss of confidence that can follow giving birth. *Managing Maternity's Newsletter 'Maternity Matters'*.

Liston-Smith, J. (2009, Spring) Maternal Leadership and the MPQ™. *Managing Maternity Newsletter 'Maternity Matters'*.

Liston-Smith, J. and Chapman, M. A. (2008, July) *Managing Maternity in Global Financial Services through Group Coaching – Unlocking the Potential Encapsulated Within 'A Black Box'*. Paper presented at Equal Opportunities International Conference, Norwich, UK.

Liston-Smith, J. and Chapman, M. A. (2009) Keeping mum in the workplace: Female leaders are discovering that the 'mothering' skills they acquire on maternity leave are also distinctly new talents critical to successful leadership. *Coaching at Work, 4*: 2.

Lucas, E. (2008) How to make a successful comeback. *Professional Manager, 17*: 28–30.

Miller, B. C. and Sollie, D. L. (1980) Normal stresses during the transition to parenthood. *Family Relations, 29*: 459–465.

Millward, L. J. (2006) The transition to motherhood in an organizational context: An interpretative phenomenological analysis. *Journal of Occupational and Organizational Psychology, 79*: 315–333.

Minuchin, P. (1988) Relationships within the family: A systems perspective on development. In R. A. Hinde and J. Stevenson-Hinde (Eds.), *Relationships within Families: Mutual Influences* (pp. 7–26). Oxford: Oxford University Press.

Minuchin, S. (1974) *Families and Family Therapy*. Cambridge, MA: Harvard University Press.

NICE (National Institute for Health and Clinical Excellence) (2007) *National Institute for Health and Clinical Excellence Clinical Guideline 45: Antenatal and Postnatal Mental Health: Clinical Management and Service Guidance*. London: NICE.

Office for National Statistics (2009, May) *ONS Statistical Bulletin*. Retrieved from http://www.statistics.gov.uk/pdfdir/bdths0509.pdf on 11 January 2010.

Palmer, S. and Szymanska, K. (2007) Cognitive behavioural coaching: An integrative approach. In S. Palmer and A. Whybrow (Eds.), *Handbook of Coaching Psychology: A Guide for Practitioners* (pp. 86–117). Hove, UK: Routledge.

Pancer, S., Pratt, M., Hunsberger, B. and Gallant, M. (2000) Thinking ahead: Complexity of expectations and the transition to parenthood. *Journal of Personality*, *68*: 253–280.

Parr, M. (1996) *Support for Couples in Transition to Parenthood*. London: University of East London.

Pawson, M. (2003) The battle with mortality and the urge to procreate. In J. Haynes and J. Miller (Eds.), *Inconceivable Conceptions – Psychological Aspects of Infertility and Reproductive Technology* (pp. 60–72). Hove, UK: Routledge.

Rosenberg, M. B. (2003) *Nonviolent Communication: A Language of Life*. Encinitas, CA: Puddle Dancer Press.

Rossi, A. S. (1968) Transition to parenthood. *Journal of Marriage and the Family*, *30*: 26–39.

Salmela-Aro, K., Nurmi, J., Saisto, T. and Halmesmaeki, E. (2000) Women's and men's personal goals during the transition to parenthood. *Journal of Family Psychology*, *14*: 171–186.

Seligman, M. and Peterson, C. (2004) *Character Strengths and Virtues: A Handbook and Classification*. Oxford: Oxford University Press.

Seligman, M. E. P., Steen, T. A., Park, N. and Peterson, C. (2005) Positive psychology progress: Empirical validation of interventions. *American Psychologist*, *60*: 410–421.

Seward, R. R. and Richter, R. (2008) International research on fathering: An expanding horizon, fathering. *Journal of Theory, Research, and Practice about Men as Fathers*, *6*: 87–91.

Shereshefsky, P. M. and Yarrow, L. J. (1973) *Psychological Aspects of a First Pregnancy and Postnatal Adaption*. New York: Raven Press.

Smith, J. A. (1999) Identity development during the transition to motherhood: An interpretative phenomenological analysis. *Journal of Reproductive and Infant Psychology*, *17*: 281–299.

Stern, D. (1995) *The Motherhood Constellation: A Unified View of Parent–Infant Psychotherapy*. London: Karnac Books.

The Children's Society (2009) *The Good Childhood Enquiry: Report Summary and The Children's Society's response*. London: The Children's Society. Retrieved from http://www.childrenssociety.org.uk/all_about_us/how_we_do_it/the_good_childhood_inquiry/report_summaries/13959.html on 12 January 2010.

von Bertalanffy, L. (1975) (E. Taschdjian (Ed.)), *Perspectives on General Systems Theory: Scientific-Philosophical Studies*. New York: George Braziller.

Wylie, M. L. (1979) The effect of expectations on the transition to parenthood. *Sociological Focus*, *12*: 323–329.

## Recommended reading

Brotherson, S. (2004, October) *The Transition from Partners to Parents: Bright Beginnings #2*. Fargo, ND: North Dakota State University Extension Service.

de Marneffe, D. (2004) *Maternal Desire: On Children, Love, and The Inner Life*. New York: Little, Brown & Co.

Parr, M. (1996) *Support for Couples in Transition to Parenthood*. London: University of East London.

Stern, D. and Bruschweiler-Stern, N. (1998) *The Birth of a Mother*. London: Bloomsbury.

# Modern mid-life

## *Emma Donaldson-Feilder and Sheila Panchal*

For many, mention of mid-life tends to evoke images of bored housewives escaping to desert islands or men swapping their family car for a flashy sports-car or motorbike! In reality, mid-life experience can be diverse. This chapter explores the opportunities and challenges of the mid-life years, and discusses how coaching can be beneficial during this transition.

There is some fuzziness about what age range actually constitutes mid-life. Levinson and associates (1978) suggest that the mid-life transition happens around age 40 years, that people enter middle adulthood at around 45 years and the culmination of middle adulthood happens around 55–60 years. However, others define mid-life as anywhere between age 30 and 60 years. As lifespans increase, the mid-point of our lives may actually be at an older age.

In popular parlance, the term 'mid-life' tends to be associated with the concept of 'mid-life crisis'. This term, coined in 1965 by Elliot Jaques and, to a large extent, made popular by Levinson (1986), refers to a period of dramatic self-doubt felt by some individuals in the middle years of life. Estimates of the likely timing of a 'mid-life crisis' suggest an average onset at age 46 years or that it happens some time after reaching 40 or 50 years (e.g. Wethington, 2000).

'Mid-life crisis' is a much-used phrase, but it appears that it may be used to refer to any period of crisis experienced in mid-life and not exclusively to crises prompted by concerns or events specific to mid-life or ageing. From a theoretical and empirical perspective, there is some controversy about whether mid-life crises really exist: there is debate about whether crisis is common in mid-life, and if a crisis occurs whether it is due to mid-life issues. Some research suggests that a mid-life crisis exists (e.g. Cierna, 1985; Levinson et al., 1978). However, others could not replicate these findings and recent research does not back it up. For example, Aldwin and Levenson (2001) report that Costa and McCrea (1980) found little evidence for increased neuroticism in mid-life. Robinson, Rosenberg and Farrell (1999) suggest that the mid-life period can be considered as a re-evaluation rather than a crisis. The term 'mid-life crisis' appears to be widely used but the range of emotional experience during this life stage is likely to vary considerably. Strenger and Ruttenberg (2008) highlighted that the notion of 'mid-life change' and associated opportunities is in fact more prevalent than the trauma of mid-life crisis. They suggest that it is important to address two myths about mid-life: that it is neither crisis (driven by acceptance of our limitations) nor transformation (based on the assumption that we are capable of boundless change). They position mid-life change as 'evolutionary' rather than 'revolutionary' and promote focusing on strengths and active self-acceptance rather than on fantasies of total transformation.

Despite challenges to the concept of 'mid-life crisis', it does seem that mid-life is a period of re-evaluation and reassessment. Current understanding suggests that mid-life, being about 'half-time' in our lives, may be a tipping point between early and later perspectives and approaches to life. It may be the point at which we start to feel that time is running out, we begin the process of accepting mortality and raise fundamental questions relating to meaning and identity. Whether associated with a specific crisis or not, transitions in this period may come from within, for example as a result of reaching a notable birthday (e.g. 40 or 50 years), or may be precipitated by external events (e.g. divorce, death of a parent, children leaving home, health issues, career peak or failure to achieve career aspirations).

If well managed, mid-life transitions can be an opportunity for positive growth and development. We may be freed from some of the responsibilities of the first half of our lives and from some of the socially constructed elements of our identity and style. This gives us a chance to discover new horizons, gain a truer sense of ourselves and invest in living the life we really want to live before reaching old age. Coaching can have a role both in supporting mid-lifers through difficult aspects of their transition and in facilitating their achievement of positive growth and development.

## Theories about the mid-life period

Jungian theory suggests that the second half of life holds the potential for the individual to go through the third phase of individuation: centring/integrating (Stein, 2006). If the person has successfully been through the prior two phases (containment/nurturance and adapting/adjusting), this stage of life is time to take on the task of becoming a centred and whole individual. Gradually abandoning the collective definitions of identity that they have been working to before, the mid-lifer can start to assume a self that emerges from within – a true inner self that is more unique and individual and less of a social construction. Jung suggests that at this point individuals are often looking for something more from life: 'Working to live and survive is no longer sufficient; one must now find something that is worth living for and this new direction must be tailor-made to fit the individual' (Stein, 2006: 211). The centring/integrating stage may also be a chance to integrate the diverse elements of one's psyche and re-integrate lost parts, acknowledging and embracing the complexity of one's whole self.

Related to the Jungian concept of the third phase of individuation in the second half of life, theory and practice around the Myers-Briggs Type Indicator (MBTI) suggest that less 'preferred' types may come more into use in mid-life as one's real/true type comes to the fore. In earlier life stages, the persona one expresses may be a mask, a social construction adopted in order to fit in with one's community and culture. By contrast, in mid-life, different aspects of personality may be explored as a sense of 'true self' emerges and an integration of different parts of the self occurs. If an individual's real/true type is different from their adopted/socially constructed type, this may precipitate a greater sense of crisis in mid-life – almost a personality shift – whereas if their persona is in line with their real type, the transition may be easier.

The influential twentieth-century psychologist Erik Erikson was a proponent of the idea that development and change occur routinely in adulthood. He mapped out eight stages of development (Erikson, 1950, 1980), each with its unique challenge or conflict between two opposing forces. The developmental aim is successfully to balance the two forces. Of the eight stages, the seventh – generativity vs. stagnation (or self-absorption) – is the one situated in mid-life. This stage focuses on the need to hand one's knowledge and experience on to future generations in order not to become self-centred and, thereby, stagnate. The eighth stage, ego integrity vs. despair, can mark the start of later life, although it may occur earlier, and concerns whether the individual can accept themselves and their life, feel a sense of community with others from different cultures and times and accept that they are just a tiny part of an enormous universe.

Coming largely from a career development perspective, Donald Super's work brought a developmental and humanistic element to a field that was, at the time, largely focused on matching people to jobs in a way that presupposed a rather static view of the individual. By contrast, Super (1965, 1980) proposed a series of life stages of growth, exploration, establishment, maintenance and decline/disengagement, although he emphasised that not all careers would or should conform to this pattern. From this perspective, the mid-life transition would be from establishment (typical ages: 25–44 years) to maintenance (typical ages: 45–64 years). Moving from a period of settling into an occupation, consolidating and advancing within it, the mid-lifer enters a period of retaining their position, updating their approach and finding new ways of doing things. However, Super also suggests that short-term cycles of change will happen, involving growth, re-exploration and re-establishment, for example during job changes and other transitions.

Daniel Levinson is probably the most specific about the ages associated with different developmental phases of life.

He divided adulthood into three eras: early (ages 15–40 years), middle (ages 40–65 years) and late (age 65 years onwards), with transitional periods between the eras and additionally at ages 30 and 50 years. Levinson thus sited the mid-life transition at around 40 years, a point of realisation that one is probably at least half-way through life, so no longer young, and of being confronted by whether one's life ambitions are going to be achieved or not. Levinson's work has been criticised for having been based on a study of men, situated in a particular era (the 1970s). However, Levinson himself acknowledges that human development will depend upon societal and cultural influences, but, drawing upon analysis of biographies spanning many centuries, posits that '. . . the basic nature and timing of life structure develop-ment are given in the life cycle . . .' (Levinson, 1986: 11).

Gilligan (1982, 1989), amongst others, has argued that women's development is rather different from men's and may not fit with the theories above, proposing instead a three-stage developmental process: caring for the self; caring for others; and recognising one's own capacity for independent action and others' responsibilities for themselves. This suggests that women may progress to emphasising relation-ship concerns less as they get older, while men's develop-ment may involve growth towards more relationship-focused concerns – with a cross-over some time in mid-life.

## Mid-life issues and opportunities

Perhaps the defining feature of mid-life transition is a growing awareness of one's own mortality and the sense that time is running out. These feelings arise for some earlier in the life cycle and can become more acute at mid-life, particu-larly if there are key ambitions that are yet to be fulfilled. It can feel like true 'make or break' time, one last chance to chase a dream. Questions around identity can be prominent, in line with Jungian and Erikson's theories: for example, 'who am I?' and 'what is my place in the world?' are questions to be addressed. Also, at mid-life people may be grappling with their place in a society where youth is valued and cele-brated, more so in the twenty-first century than ever before.

Dealing with the physical signs of ageing can be challenging for some and bring into focus issues around appearance. This may be another trigger for the re-evaluation of identity. The rapid pace of technological change can also create divisions between generations. At mid-life, people may feel left behind and in a different world from younger generations, emphasising further the loss of youth.

Despite such challenges, mid-life presents clear opportunities for positive development. Jung stated that 'the greatest potential for growth and realisation exists in the second part of life'. By gaining confidence from experience, maturity and wisdom, an individual can let go of the disappointments and insecurities associated with their younger self. It presents a true opportunity to re-evaluate and achieve in the final stages of life, with the benefits of self-acceptance and awareness. Also, the fact that fewer options may be available can be positive, as direction becomes clearer: some of the anxiety associated with overwhelming choice experienced at previous life stages can dissipate.

The current generation of mid-lifers are likely to be from the Baby Boomer generation. Baby Boomers are said to be born from 1948 to 1963 (e.g. CIPD, 2008). For this group, current cultural factors may affect their experience of mid-life. For the purposes of this discussion we will use 'Baby Boomers' as shorthand to refer to those experiencing mid-life in the current social context.

Potential changes in particular life areas will now be discussed.

### Working life/career

Many senior managers are in mid-life. Some have reached the top of their organisation or profession and may be looking for new challenges. Others may have reached a career plateau at a particular level and are faced with accepting the fact they are not likely to climb the next rung on the career ladder. In these types of situations people may change career, particularly if they have unfulfilled career passions or are keen to pursue avenues of work with greater purpose and meaning. Baby Boomers may be more likely to make a mid-life career change than previous generations, due to the increasing prevalence of portfolio careers rather than a 'job for life' mentality (Sterns and Huyck, 2001). Fewer financial demands could also make this possible. Conversely, financial demands could be at their peak for others, given costs such as children's education. For these people, the prospect of redundancy may be more stressful, particularly coupled with the perception that securing a new job is more challenging at this life stage. Recent age discrimination legislation (Age Discrimination Act 2006) is being implemented in the UK to tackle ageism in the workplace, and similar legislation exists internationally, This may address concerns for Baby Boomers.

As a result of the current global economic downturn, some Baby Boomers may be facing financial problems. The reliance on property and investments, which may not yield expected returns, and the elimination of final salary pension schemes may place some under significant financial stress.

## *Relationships*

Mid-life can be a challenging time for relationships. The 2007 data indicate that the average age of divorce in England and Wales is 43.7 years for men and 41.2 years for women (Office for National Statistics, 2008). The 'last chance saloon' mentality may apply, where those in unhappy marriages may feel it is their opportunity to leave the relationship, either to regain their independence or to seek a new partner. This may be considered to be more acceptable to Baby Boomers than prior generations, due to the general increase in divorce and less social pressure to stay married.

'Empty-nest syndrome' is associated with mid-life as children leave home (e.g. Aldwin and Levenson, 2001). There is mixed opinion on the extent of 'empty-nest' issues in the early twenty-first century, with some suggesting that the 'empty nest' may be less relevant to Baby Boomers, as their Generation X and Y children leave home later or come back to live with their parents in their 20s and even 30s due to financial pressures. Others suggest that the impact of the 'empty nest' may be more extreme for Baby Boomers, as they are the first generation to devote so much time and attention to raising their offspring. They have been termed 'helicopter parents', who hover over their children even as they reach adulthood.

Where the 'empty nest' does occur in mid-life, it can affect marriages for better or worse. For some it is a positive change, giving parents a chance to refresh their relationship without the daily demands of children. It can create time and freedom. People may travel, explore new career options, invest in friendships and pursue new interests. For others it can be disorientating, affecting their identity both as individuals and as a couple who no longer have a common purpose.

In terms of the direct impact of an 'empty nest', women who have played a significant parenting role, which is likely for Baby Boomers, can feel a great sense of loss at their children leaving home. For male Baby Boomers, the man's role may be more akin to the traditional breadwinner than for younger generations; when children leave home, these men may reflect on their parental role and feel a sense of regret at not having given more time to their families.

Some will become grandparents in mid-life. Baby Boomers may put more time and effort into their grandparenting role than previous generations, as increasing numbers of Generation X and Y parents are both working. This is a chance for mid-lifers to approach the parenting role more in the way that they might have wanted to with their own children, without the pressures of new parenthood. Being an active grandparent also connects to an important theme at mid-life, which is that of legacy, meaning and community. As this theme comes to the fore, individuals may find themselves looking for ways to 'give back' to others and pass on their wisdom to younger generations.

Parental illness or death becomes more common in mid-life. This means that some, perhaps particularly women, take on caring responsibilities for parents or other elderly family members. Himes (1994) indicated that half of women with a surviving parent at mid-life spend at least some time in a caregiving role. This can be a positive role as well as a challenging one. Some Baby Boomers may find their caring role covering an extended period, due to children staying at home longer combined with parents living longer. For others, their caring responsibilities may be significantly reduced, given the increase in women not having children, through choice or otherwise, and the opportunities for older people to stay healthy for longer. Losing parents, spouses or other loved ones at this life stage may enhance the focus on mortality that mid-life brings anyway, prompting changes that the individual may not have pursued otherwise.

Other social trends may influence Baby Boomer relationships in mid-life; for example, stepfamilies are more prevalent than in the past, which can present both opportunities and challenges. Also, Baby Boomers may experience less continuity of relationships over their lifespan as a result of more dispersed families and greater social mobility. This can become an issue as mid-life concerns around connection and community become more pressing.

## *Health*

Health issues are likely to become a feature at mid-life. Maintaining a healthy lifestyle may become a priority, and one that is potentially more challenging with ageing. This is the time when women will experience the menopause, with variable impact: some may be affected emotionally as they reflect on their lost fertility (e.g. Sheehy, 1992). The male menopause also has physical and emotional implications. Baby Boomers are likely to be in a better position to understand, prevent and address health issues such as the menopause, as there is significant information available to them via a range of channels and facilitated by technology. In addition, health coaching has increasingly become available in the UK and USA and other countries too, which assists coachees in achieving their health-related goals (see Palmer, Tubbs and Whybrow, 2003).

In summary, mid-life presents a range of challenges and opportunities. Deep identity transformations can occur, and circumstantial changes can also prompt development. The next section will review how coaching can be an effective intervention to help people navigate this life stage.

## Coaching at mid-life

Given the demographics of senior management, those of us providing executive coaching services are likely to be working with at least some coachees who are in mid-life. As we have seen, not all those in mid-life will be in transition and not all transitions in mid-life are due specifically to mid-life issues. However, having an understanding of the transitional and developmental issues that may arise in mid-life can give an additional depth and utility to coaching people in this period of their life.

Coaching may be a particularly influential intervention in mid-life, as it can help to address the transpersonal issues that may be arising for the coachee, relating to meaning, purpose, values and identity, together with the need to accept reality and handle loss (lost hopes and dreams, as well as more tangible losses). At the same time, coaching can normalise the turmoil that a coachee may be experiencing and 'hold' the chaos and confusion brought about by transitions and mid-life crises. It can also address more pragmatic issues relating to lifestyle and health that may arise in this life phase.

### *Meaning, purpose, values and identity*

As identified above, mid-life events can lead individuals to question who they are and what their lives are about. Coaching can provide the space for coachees to reassess and re-evaluate. Exercises and discussion in coaching can facilitate coachees to address the following issues:

- **Search for meaning and purpose**. Coaching can be an ideal space in which to support a process of evaluating what the coachee's life is about. Transpersonal approaches and exercises on meaning and purpose can help individuals to consider what they would like their legacy to be, what they want their life to have been about and 'who I want to be'. Often, this will involve explicit or implicit exploration of the individual's values.
- **Identity and self-acceptance**. Coaching can also allow individuals to build self-awareness and self-acceptance

and explore any changes in 'self' brought about by mid-life transitions. This may include:

o **Personality tests**. While many senior executives will already have taken a range of personality tests, for others an exploration of their personality will be a new concept. Even those who have completed such tests in the past may look at themselves in a new light as a result of their mid-life transition and the potential for the 'true self' to emerge at this point. As mentioned above, results from tools such as the MBTI may show a different type emerging, one that is potentially closer to the true self. This can be a chance to disentangle the true self from the persona adopted in earlier life phases – particularly if the latter has been a social construction that does not fit completely with the true self – and to explore and integrate different aspects of self.

o **Feedback**. Provision of 360° feedback, revealing the perceptions of others, can offer an opportunity for the coachee to reflect on 'who am I being' as compared with 'who I want to be' and potentially 'who am I when I am truly myself'.

o **Life roles**. It may also be helpful to identify the range of roles the individual is playing in different parts of their life (and how these are shifting as a result of mid-life transitions). Linked to exploring values, this may help the individual to consider how their identity plays out in the different domains of life and whether they are being true to their value system.

o **Strengths**. Taking a strengths-based coaching approach can be a powerful way to help the individual see what they have to offer and provide a firm base on which to build future development.

• **Sense-making and paradox**. As well as exploring values, meaning and identity, coaching in mid-life may also be a place for the individual to confront existential issues and paradoxes such as meaning versus lack of meaning and the real self versus the ideal self.

## *Mindfulness, acceptance and being in the moment*

At the same time as helping the coachee to explore transpersonal and conceptual issues, coaching in mid-life may also be an opportunity to ground the individual in the moment-by-moment aspects of existence. For those who have been striving to achieve and whose lives have been full of busyness, mid-life may be the moment at which they wish to relinquish 'automatic pilot' and be really present in their own life. Mindfulness exercises and learning to 'be in the moment' can be a powerful way to facilitate this kind of shift.

For individuals who have spent much of their time either worrying about the future or ruminating on the past, the revelation of being present *now* can help to make dramatic shifts in mood and stress levels. Learning a more mindful way of being can help the coachee to deal with the pain and loss that mid-life transitions often bring, including loss of dreams and plans that become less likely or impossible to realise. It can help with the moment-by-moment experience of uncomfortable emotions and build a more accepting approach to difficulties.

Combined with a greater clarity about values, purpose and identity, mindfulness can be a means of striking a balance between 'seeking/getting what I want' and striving to 'be who I want to be', while at the same time 'accepting/ wanting what I get' and being realistic and honest about 'who I am, who I am not and who I can never be'. The compassion towards self and others engendered by the practice of mindfulness can be a mechanism for helping those in mid-life deal with these issues. Together with positive psychology tools relating to appreciation and gratitude, this can be a powerful way to help individuals lift themselves out of critical and negative states.

At the same time, mindfulness can contribute to helping individuals make choices that are better aligned with their values, purpose and identity. By facilitating people to be more present in the moment that they make decisions and take action, mindfulness allows people to respond thoughtfully rather than reacting in a 'knee-jerk' way that is not in tune with their value system.

## Coaching as 'holding' and normalising transitional uncertainty

When coaching coachees who are going through a mid-life transition, coaches may find themselves 'holding' considerable turmoil and confusion. The classic transitional states of chaos and uncertainty, whether change is thrust upon the individual or emerges from within, can take time to resolve – time in the 'neutral zone' (Bridges, 1995). The coach may need to role-model being with this discomfort and give the coachee permission to be in this state; coaching may be a delicate balance, helping the coachee to find some structure without forcing structure where the person is not ready.

Coaching may also play a part in normalising the turmoil of mid-life transitions. By reflecting on human transitions, coaching can foster acceptance of change as normal and positive. It can help the coachee to recognise that change is a fluid process and there will be chaos and confusion, facilitating a shift from thinking that there is something wrong to seeing the discomfort as quite normal.

## Lifestyle and health

On a pragmatic note, as mid-life may bring health issues to the fore, coaching may also be a chance for those in mid-life to address healthy lifestyle issues in order to prevent potential future health problems. For example, it may cover issues such as:

- smoking cessation
- sensible alcohol consumption
- exercise and activity
- healthy eating
- relaxation, including meditation, taking breaks, holidays, etc.

For some, coaching may be a way of addressing assertiveness issues, helping coachees to assert their needs and to be willing to take care of and have time for themselves. Attending coaching may itself be part of this, in as much as attending coaching involves the coachee setting time aside for him/herself. This may be particularly pertinent for those who have been in parenting and caring roles, where they have not focused on their own well-being.

Of course, coaching is not the only source of support for coachees in mid-life: other channels, such as support and interest groups, may be helpful. Role models and mentors can also play an invaluable role.

As with any coaching encounter that involves issues of identity and emotional well-being, coaching individuals in mid-life carries the risk of getting into some fundamental and/or psychodynamic areas. It is vital that the coach be conscious of the boundaries between coaching and counselling/psychotherapy, that they guard against straying beyond the coaching remit by identifying when they reach the limits of coaching and referring the coachee for counselling/psychotherapy if appropriate. Good supervision is important to help the coach reflect on these boundary issues.

## Case study

Bill[1] was a senior manager in his late 40s who had recently had a month's sickness absence due to stress-related health problems: his GP signed him off due to symptoms of exhaustion, anxiety and depression. Following a meeting towards the end of his sick-leave, his employer's Occupational Health advisor reported that he was fit to return to work, but recommended that he get some support to deal with the workplace issues that contributed to his health problems. His HR manager suggested executive coaching and arranged for him to see me (first author, E.D.-F.). My HR client explained that the company valued Bill highly and recognised that work may have contributed to his recent health problems; however, she also felt that Bill was struggling with non-work issues and was not good at managing his own stress levels.

At the first coaching session, we explored Bill's current situation and the issues on which he wished to work in coaching. The following information emerged:

- Prior to his sick-leave, Bill's line manager, one of the company's top managers, had subjected Bill to some particularly harsh and undermining behaviour. Perhaps threatened by Bill's success, this manager had a tendency to criticise Bill in front of colleagues and pick up on any minor errors he made. The manager had marked Bill down in a recent performance appraisal and blocked a recent promotion application. The manager was now under investigation for bullying and Bill's reporting line had been switched to a new person.
- Over the past year, Bill had divorced his wife of 20 years and was still in conflict with her regarding finances and contact with their two school-age children. He had recently started a relationship with a woman he had met through friends. Meanwhile, Bill's mother died 6 months ago, quite suddenly, and his father was struggling to cope on his own. As an only child, Bill felt a sense of great responsibility for supporting his father both practically and emotionally.
- Bill felt he had lost his sense of direction in recent years. Having spent much of his career striving for the next promotion, he was now unsure whether he wanted to rise any higher in the organisation – or whether he even wanted to stay in the same field. He yearned for a sense of meaning and purpose that seemed lacking in his current line of work. However, he was conscious that he needed to stay in a well-paid job in order to be able to support his ex-wife and children financially, which meant that he felt 'trapped' in his work for at least the next 5–10 years.
- Despite appearing confident and being known as a 'straight talker' who was unafraid of conflict, Bill actually spent a lot of the time wracked with self-doubt. He was extremely adept at 'giving himself a hard time' and constantly afraid of failure. No matter how many times he succeeded, he always feared that the next project would be a disaster and he would be 'found out' for the incompetent person he felt himself to be.
- Bill was not sure whether his stress-related health problems were partly caused by his feelings of lack of direction or whether the period of sickness absence, by giving him time to question his situation, had been part of the reason

why he lost his sense of purpose. He acknowledged that he was not particularly good at looking after his health or work–life balance, rarely finding time to take exercise and inclined to work late more often than not. Worrying about work was disrupting his sleep, and the resultant fatigue was making everything seem harder to handle.

By the end of the initial session, we agreed that we could work together in coaching and that the coaching process would have dual aims:

- to help Bill explore how to get a greater sense of meaning, purpose and direction in his work in particular, but also in his life more generally; and
- to help him find ways of being both psychologically and physically healthier despite the range of stressors in his life.

To support these two tracks, Bill agreed to undertake two exercises in preparation for our second session: to spend some time thinking about 'who he wanted to be' in different areas of his life (career, relationships, parenting, family, friends, community, leisure, spirituality); and to keep a diary of how he was spending his time in an 'average' week. Over the course of eight further coaching sessions, we built on these exercises through discussion and further activities.

*Values and purpose*

Bill used the initial exercise about 'who he wanted to be', and further exercises exploring his values and purpose, to develop a rich sense of what mattered to him in the different parts of his life. He ranked the different areas in terms of priority and scored the extent to which he was currently living according to his values in each area. This helped him to clarify that being a good father to his children and developing a good relationship with his new partner were his top priorities, but that maintaining a high quality of work was still important for his self-esteem. It also revealed that he was not currently living according to his values. For example, because he was feeling under pressure from work and from dealing with his father's situation, he tended to be grumpy and distracted when he saw his children and not to find quality time for his new relationship. This recognition was the first step to helping him shift his approach.

### Healthy lifestyle and being 'in the moment'

Review of Bill's diary of his average week showed that he spent a lot of his time rushing from one activity to the next, worrying about what he needed to do next or ruminating over what he had just done. He was rarely fully present in the moment and lived a lot of his life on 'automatic pilot'. Meanwhile, his 'self-talk' was in overdrive, giving himself a hard time about what he did (or did not do) and echoing the criticisms of his former line manager as 'evidence' that he was a failure. That he was not exercising, eating healthily or managing his work–life boundaries effectively were further sources of self-criticism.

We spent considerable time over the next few sessions discussing how Bill could be kinder to himself in terms of how he spent his time and, more importantly, in terms of his attitude to himself. While we agreed that building more exercise, good nutrition and relaxation into his diary was important, we also came to the conclusion that this could only happen if he could shift his approach: paradoxically, in order to fit more in, he needed to slow down. Using a range of mindfulness-based exercises, Bill explored ways of being more 'in the moment': paying attention to what was actually happening as it happened; recognising his thoughts and feelings as passing phenomena that did not necessarily need to determine his behaviour; learning to ground himself through bringing attention to his breathing or the sensations in his body. This gave him greater choice about what to do in situations rather than responding automatically, facilitating healthier choices and clearer boundaries. It also enabled him to recognise the negative self-talk at an earlier stage and not to 'buy in' to it as much as in the past.

### Using being 'in the moment' to live a values-based life

The big advantage of combining mindfulness approaches with exploration of values and purpose was that being more 'in the moment' allowed Bill to make more conscious choices about how to spend his time and the approach he was taking, thereby enabling him to choose actions and approaches based on his values.

## Difficulties encountered

- While the brief description above makes the process of exploring values and purpose seem linear and straightforward, in fact it was much more 'messy' than this. Initially, Bill struggled to express 'who he wanted to be' and had to revisit these exercises a number of times before he was happy with the outcome. In this liminal phase, he found it difficult to see any meaning and several times reported feeling 'lost' or 'stuck'. Thus the coaching sessions had to 'hold' considerable uncertainty, chaos and confusion. At times, it felt as if the coaching process itself and I as the coach were getting 'lost' and 'stuck'. Good supervision was important to help me not to get drawn into the confusion or feel deskilled by it. Good supervision was also important to ensure that I maintained a clear boundary around the coaching work and did not stray into more 'therapeutic' domains.

- For a coachee like Bill who was highly self-critical, there was a risk that discovering that he was not living according to his values could be yet another source of self-criticism. It was therefore important to provide a supportive, non-critical approach to the process, building compassion into the exercises and discussions. However, there was a delicate balance to be struck between taking this compassionate approach whilst also being challenging enough to support and motivate change in behaviour and attitude.

- Although he recognised that his self-criticism was harsh and could be destructive, Bill also struggled to let go of it. He saw it as the source of his success and he reasoned that if he hadn't given himself a hard time he would never have been driven to achieve all he had achieved. We spent considerable time exploring how he might motivate himself in future without resorting to negative self-talk.

- As a senior manager, Bill was very busy and under a lot of pressure. He found it hard to make time for coaching sessions and to do the exercises between sessions. At the start, he postponed a couple of sessions and either did not do the exercises or did not do them completely. Again, I had to find a balance between, on the one hand, role-modelling compassion/kindness and not increasing the pressure on him and on the other, helping him explore how to make coaching, and his personal development, a priority.
- A pragmatic, action-based man, Bill initially struggled with the concept of mindfulness. He was inclined to dismiss some of the exercises as being too 'airy fairy' for him, so I needed to de-mystify the concept and talk in very concrete and pragmatic terms about the difference between being in the moment and being on automatic pilot. Quoting recent research on the benefits of mindfulness also helped.

## Discussion issues

1  Is a crisis more likely in mid-life than in other life phases? If so, why?
2  Which issues are unique to mid-life, if any?
3  Can a coach who has not yet reached mid-life effectively coach coachees through mid-life transitions?

## Endnote

1  Note that Bill is not a real person. He is an amalgamation of facets of a number of different coachees with whom I (E.D.-F.) have had the pleasure to work in recent years.

## References

Aldwin, C. M. and Levenson, M. R. (2001) Stress, coping and health at midlife. In M. E. Lachman (Ed.), *Handbook of Mid-Life Development* (pp. 188–214). New York: John Wiley.

Bridges, W. (1995) *Managing Transitions: Making the Most of Change*. London: Nicholas Brealey Publishing.

Cierna, J. R. (1985) Death concern and businessmen's mid-life crisis. *Psychological Reports*, 56: 83–87.

CIPD (Chartered Institute of Personnel and Development) (2008) *Gen Up: How the Four Generations Work*. London: CIPD. Retrieved from http://www.cipd.co.uk/onlineinfodocuments on 10 January 2009.

Costa, P. T. and McCrae, R. R. (1980) Influence of extraversion and neuroticism on subjective well-being: Happy and unhappy people. *Journal of Personality and Social Psychology*, *38*: 668–678.

Erikson, E. (1950) *Childhood and Society*. New York: Norton.

Erikson, E. (1980) *Identity and the Life-Cycle*. New York: Norton.

Gilligan, C. (1982) *In a Different Voice*. Boston, MA: Harvard University Press.

Gilligan, C. (1989) *Mapping the Moral Domain: A Contribution of Women's Thinking to Psychological Theory and Education*. Boston, MA: Harvard University Press.

Himes C. L. (1994) Parental caregiving by adult women: A demographic perspective. *Research on Aging*, *16*: 191–211.

Jacques, E. (1965) Death and the midlife crisis. *International Journal of Psychoanalysis*, *46*: 502–514.

Levinson, D. J. (1986) A conception of adult development. *American Psychologist*, *41*: 3–13.

Levinson, D. J., Darrow, C. N., Klein, E. B., Levinson, M. H. and McKee, B. (1978) *The Seasons in a Man's Life*. New York: Knopf.

Office for National Statistics (2008, August) *News Release – Divorce Rates Lowest for 26 Years*. Retrieved from http://www.statistics.gov.uk/pdfdir/div0808.pdf on 8 January, 2010.

Palmer, S., Tubbs, I. and Whybrow, W. (2003) Health coaching to facilitate the promotion of healthy behaviour and achievement of health-related goals. *International Journal of Health Promotion and Education*, *41*: 91–93.

Robinson, S. D., Rosenberg, H. J. and Farrell, M. P. (1999) The midlife crisis revisited. In S. L. Willis and J. D. Reid (Eds.), *Life in the Middle: Psychological and Social Development in Middle Age* (pp. 47–77). San Diego, CA: Academic Press.

Sheehy, G. (1992) *The Silent Passage*. London: Random House.

Stein, M. (2006) Individuation. In R. K. Papadopoulos (Ed.), *The Handbook of Jungian Psychology: Theory, Practice and Applications* (pp. 196–214). Hove, UK: Routledge.

Sterns, H. and Huyck, M. H. (2001) The role of work in midlife. In M. E. Lachman (Ed.), *Handbook of Mid-Life Development* (pp. 447–486). New York: Wiley.

Strenger, S. and Ruttenberg, A. (2008). The existential necessity of mid-life change. *Harvard Business Review*, *86*: 82–90.

Super, D. (1965) A theory of vocational development. *American Development*, *8*: 185–90.

Super, D. E. (1980) A life span, life space approach to career development. *Journal of Vocational Behavior*, *13*: 282–298.
Wethington, E. (2000) Expecting stress: Americans and the mid-life
crisis. *Motivation and Emotion*, *24*: 85–103.

## Recommended reading

Lachman, M. E. (Ed.) (2001) *Handbook of Mid-Life Development*.
New York: Wiley.
Strenger, S. and Ruttenberg, A. (2008) The existential necessity of
mid-life change. *Harvard Business Review*, *86*: 82–90.

# Looking forward to retirement

## *Siobhain O'Riordan*

There are a number of challenges facing us when we attempt to define and characterise retirement as a life-stage transition. Broadly speaking, the modern-day society in which we live might be considered to be focused, at least to some extent, upon age and physical appearance. This has played a part in influencing the development and reinforcement of a number of popularly held stereotypes for different life stages. For retirement, these tend to be based upon our beliefs and assumptions about changes associated with people growing older and our understanding of generic routes both toward and post-retirement. The nature of retirement as a transition and experience is complex, multi-faceted and can be influenced by a number of factors. Incorporating aspects of our lives such as family, relationships, finances, health and social circumstances, this suggests that treatment of retirement in terms of 'age' or simply as an 'event', scheduled to happen at the end of our working life, is somewhat limiting. To fully understand retirement as a life-stage transition, a comprehensive consideration should ideally incorporate the multi-dimensional nature of this process as well as individual experiences of adjustment (e.g. McGoldrick and Cooper, 1994).

Ways in which we might describe retirement include: retiring from full-time paid employment; the end of our career and work activities; the drawing of a state pension; or perhaps a continuation of the lifespan with new opportunities. A description was provided by Atchley (1988), who considered lack of employment for the period of a year (or all year) and the collection of retirement benefit to be key factors in the definition of retirement. When we review the literature we can see that early definitions have tended to be based on economic principles: Latulippe (1996), for example, defines retirement in terms of an individual who has stopped being active economically. Whilst simplistic, such straightforward definitions and descriptions may be criticised for not fully accounting for individual differences and experiences.

The far-reaching significance of retirement has been acknowledged in some explanations at both an individual and a societal level. During a consideration of the behavioural dimensions of retirement economics, Aaron (1999: v) argues that: 'Retirement stands as one of the most important economic, psychological and social transitions in most people's lives'. An economic view of retirement by Burtless (1999: 7) supports this conceptualisation: 'Retirement is an event with profound personal, social and economic consequences'. Explanations, definitions, theories and models of retirement can also be drawn from other areas of the literature, such as sociology, psychology and gerontology, thus making a significant contribution and furthering our understanding of retirement as a life-stage transition. A problem with this extensive offering is that it provides a general lack of consensus in terms of definitions and research focus, although integration of the theories and findings from these allied professions can to some extent provide us with a comprehensive consideration of retirement as a life-stage transition.

The nature of what we mean by retirement in Western society is dynamic and continually changing. This further adds to the difficulties in specifically setting out characterisations for this life stage. A number of themes may be linked to this fluidity, such as: early retirement; changes to the concept of mandatory retirement; increased work-related opportunities post-retirement; and shifting perceptions in how as a society we view 'old age'. Types of exit from the workforce into retirement that individuals experience in modern societies also vary and seem to be becoming more flexible over time. With early retirement on the increase in many countries (e.g. Aaron, 1999; McGoldrick and Cooper, 1988), the number of people reaching mandatory retirement is declining. Exits from the workforce at this time could be planned, unplanned, through choice or forced. Whilst some individuals retire early, some of us work on until mandatory retirement, with yet others choosing to continue to work into later life. The actual transition between work and retirement may also vary, with some individuals making an immediate transition in comparison to those who undertake a gradual decline in working hours over a period of time. Such dynamic shifts also further complicate the development of a clear definition of retirement and may have implications for the boundaries between our understanding of pre-retirement and post-retirement. Because of this array of factors and the multi-dimensionality of retirement, it is possible to see the appeal of adopting a straightforward approach via the use of economic principles as a basis for defining retirement as a life-stage transition.

Today, potentially the most significant influencing factor upon retirement as a life-stage transition is what appears to be our ever-increasing longevity. For many of us living in wealthier modern countries, when we retire we can anticipate living more than 20 years within a stage of the life course that also tends to be healthier (Rowe and Kahn, 1998). For the UK it has been suggested that 'By 2020, half the population of the UK will be aged 50 and over' (Department for Work and Pensions, 2009) and for what appears to be the first time in the UK the number of people above state pension age has recently become greater than those aged below 16 years (Office for National Statistics, 2008). Additionally, it has been predicted that there will be approximately three people of working age in comparison to each person above state pension age by 2032 (Office for National Statistics, 2008: 20). However, in the UK there is currently the possibility that the government will bring forward plans to delay the state retirement age for both males and females. As well as broader societal consequences, these earlier than anticipated plans are also likely to have particular implications for the retirement preparation of the first cohort of people impacted by this increase to the state pensionable age.

European statistics tell us that at the beginning of the twenty-first century one in four Europeans were 60 years old and above, whereas in 2050 demographic estimates suggest that over a third of Europeans will be 60 years old plus (Fernández-Ballesteros and Caprara, 2003). These statistics have led to the suggestion that '. . . all sciences and professions concerned with the aging phenomenon will have an obligation to contribute to increasing the quality of life and well-being of these millions of people' (Fernández-Ballesteros and Caprara, 2003: 129). Birren (2000: 13) proposed that: 'Psychologists as scientists and professionals should study not only the dynamics of extended life expectancy, but also the issue of how the gift of long life may be used'. If we look ahead to a society where people are living longer and longer, an implication of this is that we will encounter an ever-increasing ageing population and, over time, this is likely to influence our definitions and characterisations of work, pre-retirement and retirement.

When considering retirement as a life-stage transition it is worthwhile noting that although the concept of what it means to grow older in today's Western society is changing, people's experiences often still vary dramatically. Positive opportunities and experiences are often offered in middle to later life. However, on balance there are also a number of common sources of challenges and difficulties. As academics and practitioners working in this field we should also appreciate that historical, political, cultural and gender influences are all important and defining factors in terms of how we characterise what we mean by retirement in a modern society. In the light of this it is useful and reflective to consider retirement, at a minimum, as a life-stage transition set within an individual's developmental, generational and cultural context.

## Theoretical considerations and generational factors

As we look forward to retirement, issues associated with growing old represent the most obvious differentiating factors in comparison to other life-stage transitions. Whilst some characteristics may be identified as specific to retirement as a life transition, others are shared and may be experienced when managing other life milestones such as 'turning thirty'. Thus, it also seems likely that experiences from one transition may impact upon and prepare us for others at different points in our lives. Based on current generational factors and the gift of increasing life expectancy, the retirement revolution may be changing the shape of modern society in a number of ways, particularly if we are to accept that the current cohort of retirees has potentially greater opportunities and choice than those from previous generations.

Existing psychological and allied theories and research can inform our understanding of retirement, relevant generational factors and our work within this coaching context. Research and theory relevant to this life transition includes lifespan development stage theories (e.g. Erikson, 1968; Levinson et al., 1978), life course perspectives (e.g. Kim and Moen, 2001), role theory, continuity theory, life events theories (Holmes and Rahe, 1967), transition theories, positive psychology and theories of adjustment to old age. Alongside the retirement literature, relevant research studies can also be drawn from a number of other areas, including studies looking at goal-setting across the adult life span, subjective well-being, the developmental and social context of the retirement experience, coping, work and redundancy. However, there are a number of problems with retirement and related research, namely methodological issues such as cohort effects, the general lack of longitudinal research, a limited focus on contextual factors, the tendency to use all male samples and issues relating to the generalisation of findings. In addition, the pre-retirement experience in many cases has been overlooked in the existing research and the applicability of existing retirement theories to the experience of women is questionable.

There are a number of life areas relevant, but not exclusive, to this life-stage transition. Some of these are considered in greater detail throughout this chapter in relation to the challenges, opportunities, questions and characteristics of individuals at this particular age in today's society:

- relationships, family and friends
- work and career
- finances
- health
- lifestyle.

At this point, it is relevant to further emphasise the view that it is unlikely that there are such things as a generic route or specific patterns in retirement. It is also noteworthy that whilst broad differences between generational groupings can be useful (e.g. the Silent Generation, Traditionalists, Baby Boomers), these can also be unhelpful as they may present snapshot characterisations of these cohorts of people that ignore important themes and individual differences both within and between generations. Increased life expectancy, mobility, consumerism and choice are all potential generational factors specific to the current cohort of retirees in a modern Western society. When viewing some of these generational factors in this light, it does seem to suggest that retirement as we know it today may be a relatively new concept. This proposal does introduce implications regarding the extent to which some theories, models and research findings are able to contribute to our understanding of retirement as a life-stage transition.

## *Relationships, family and friends*

As the retirement revolution impacts in economic, social and political terms it is having a noticeable influence upon our personal relationships and the structure of the family. For some, 'empty-nest' syndrome, grandparenting responsibilities or greater dependency from ageing parents, friends or one's life partner are all life circumstances that may impact upon retirement planning and experiences post-retirement. To support this latter point, figures for the UK have quite recently revealed that 2.8 million people aged 50 years and above provide unpaid care (Office for National Statistics, 2005). In the home, adjustment to previously defined domestic roles and changes in the division of labour regarding household activities may also take place as one or both partners retire. Changes to relationships during the transition from work to retirement may also include immediate and/or gradual detachment from friends and colleagues, either through choice or as a result of factors that contribute to the social isolation of the retiree. Alternatively, increased mobility, freedom and social opportunities in today's retirement might mean that we actually broaden our people network. Theories on adjustment to old age, such as social disengagement theory (Cumming and Henry, 1961) and social activity theory (Havighurst, Neugarten and Tobin, 1968), are still useful today and can help to explain our level of social engagement and activities as we get older.

The family may have an important role to play during the decision-making that occurs during retirement and this may have been overlooked to some extent in the existing literature (Lundberg, 1999). Research has examined the role of influences such as the family and personal relationships (Henkens, 1999; Szinovacz, DeViney and Davey, 2001) in regard to the retirement decision-making process. Henkens' (1999) findings suggested that early retirement decisions may be considered to be due to influences within the home, particularly in regard to married men's early retirement decisions. It has also been suggested that women may tend to retire for different reasons to men and this includes the desire to fulfil the role of caregiver (Richardson, 1993). Szinovacz, DeViney and Davey (2001) found that the influence of the family during retirement decisions differed on the basis of gender, race and marital status.

## Work and career

The literature leads us to believe that work is a major part of the adult life course. Some theorists argue that, due to the loss of the worker role at retirement, people often struggle to re-define their self-identity and status, particularly if this has been based on previously held work-related factors such as job role, employment status, level of responsibility and income. With the removal of this worker role and the introduction of labels such as retiree, senior citizen or pensioner it is perhaps understandable why the loss of some aspects of our personal status, associated with retirement, might be viewed somewhat negatively. It is also relevant to comment though that many retirees participate in unpaid or voluntary work and a positive benefit of the retirement revolution is the significant contribution that the retired workforce continues to make within this sector of our modern communities.

Such transferability of existing work-based skills may also play a part at a personal level to the individual's adjustment over time, particularly when they view their worker role as important. The significance of the continuation between work and retirement has been supported by those highlighting that good adjustment can depend on meaningful activities and maintaining the same level of participation in valued activities in retirement as was present on the previous job (e.g. Atchley, 1976, 1982a, 1982b; Braithwaite and Gibson, 1987; Friedmann and Havighurst, 1954). There is also some further support for the potential relevance of our working life to our retirement experience, suggesting that individuals bring an occupationally learned approach with them into this major life transition that can play a part in shaping their course through retirement (Moen, 1996). Thus, it seems that it may be more appropriate and helpful to consider retirement from the perspective of continuity of our life course rather than a brand new stage of our lives that begins post-work, especially when we note that employment and retirement experiences may also differ on the basis of factors such as gender, culture, health and individual differences.

## *Finances*

Until the recent downturn of the global economy the current generation of retirees were seen to be benefiting financially from the housing boom and inheriting property, although this should be set in the appropriate context as some retirees have also been experiencing financial difficulties for some time, including issues relating to pension shortfalls or problems maintaining standards of living post-retirement. More and more people are working into retirement, both paid and voluntarily, and this appears to be for a variety of different reasons such as interest, social engagement or for financial necessity. Whilst we are perhaps seeing a growing trend where redundancy in later life is becoming the new retirement, this also has potentially negative consequences for both the individual and society. Such an occurrence is likely to have major effects on financial decision-making for these individuals and may require the development of new strategies and retirement planning. Research has tended to suggest that there is little relationship between subjective well-being and economic factors (Diener and Diener, 1996) and that, in respect of retirement, subjective well-being does not decline as a result of constraints or a drop in income – there are other factors such as activity, leisure opportunities, the family and health that may be more influential (e.g. Beck and Page, 1988; Lowenstein, Prelec and Weber, 1999). However, such findings should be considered within the context of the general limitations of research in this field.

## *Health*

Physical changes associated with growing older and increased risk of age-related illnesses over time are potential challenges faced by us all at this later time in our lives. Dependent upon the reason why individuals retire from the workforce, health may have a different role to play. It has been recognised that the context and relationships within which one retires are important, which suggests that individuals who retire due to health grounds must adapt not only to retirement but also to the changing life circumstances that are introduced because of their own or another's medical condition (e.g. Kim and Moen, 2002). In terms of our own health there are also a number of characteristics that make retirement comparable with redundancy as a type of job loss. If we examine earlier work that has looked at individuals who retire early through no choice of their own, perhaps because of redundancy or health reasons, or they are not prepared for the retirement experience, we see that they may experience similar stages to those for redundancy, such as boredom, depression and loneliness (Cooper, 1979).

A broad review of the existing literature suggests that retirement has not been shown to have a predictable negative effect on physical health, self-esteem, life satisfaction or mental health (e.g. Nadelson, 1969) and that researchers are now starting to examine factors that may be involved in positive attitudes to retirement (e.g. Atchley, 1976; Mutran, Reitzes and Fernandez, 1997). Research focusing upon aspects of positive ageing and well-being throughout the lifespan has also found that happiness is approximately U-shaped through the life course, whereas mental distress tends to reach a maximum in middle age (Blanchflower and Oswald, 2008). However, more research is needed to identify the complexity and the factors that influence the relationship between psychological well-being and quality of life.

## *Lifestyle*

Currently, a popular-held view of retirement is that it is a 'golden era'. However, the extent to which retirement as a life transition is a normative process, a period of crisis or perhaps somewhere 'in between' can be challenged. The literature suggests that there is little consistent evidence of a general retirement crisis (e.g. Beck, 1982; Mayring, 2000; Nadelson, 1969; Palmore et al., 1985), although there has been evidence to suggest that as many as one-third of people will experience some difficulties in adjusting post-retirement (Bosse et al., 1991; Braithwaite and Gibson, 1987) and will actually undergo a decrease in life satisfaction as a result of the transition (e.g. Elwell and Maltbie-Crannell, 1981). Following removal of the work infrastructure, difficulties relating to time and self-management can have an impact upon lifestyles. However, opportunities and choice for modern retirees include geographical mobility, flexibility of lifestyles, social and leisure options and work, which may be paid and unpaid. In addition there are choices related to travel, second careers, lifestyle and educational opportunities. Trends in the reason for retirement have been reported as changing over time and Burtless (1999) argued that there is an increase in the reasons given for retirement in terms of the pursuit of leisure activities or through personal choice. The literature has also shown us relationships between goal directedness and life satisfaction, as well as with well-being, adjustment and other factors associated with healthy development (Payne, Robbins and Dougherty, 1991; Smith and Robbins, 1989), thus emphasising a potential role for coaching.

## Coaching

What are the key factors that have led to the emergence of retirement and third-age coaching? It has already been highlighted that people are spending 20 or more years in retirement and there has been a move by employers towards facilitating 'exit strategies', both as a duty of care to the individual and for the purpose of minimising the impact on the organisation when the person retires. This practice is of course not new and has previously involved a variety of different sources of support – retirement workshops, retirement counselling and one-to-one practical/financial advice. Retirement coaching moves outside of the 'financial planning box', which is often, but not always, a primary focus of many alternative options. In comparison to some of these other types of available help, the purpose of coaching is not to provide a prescribed formula for retirement success but instead to offer a flexible approach that is tailored around the coachee's agenda, although arguably from a practical viewpoint it is preferable for retirement coaches to be able to demonstrate awareness and have insight into retirement, business and related lifestyle issues.

Retirement coaching programmes vary and there are also a number of different settings in which coaching can take place, which include face-to-face and telephone formats. With the increase in modern technology, retirement coaching can also be undertaken online via a variety of different media. Timeframes might be set up around a short coaching programme, coaching over longer periods of time, occasional (as and when) sessions and/or as part of other initiatives. Whilst this type of work might involve one-to-one coaching, there is also the scope for workshops for both individuals and groups and as part of broader coaching and non-coaching initiatives. For example, couples coaching might be particularly relevant during this life stage when there are issues relating to domestic relationships and roles.

When considering retirement as a life-stage transition there appears to be a number of purposes for coaching, the most specific of which is to facilitate the coachee towards making the complex aspects of their retirement more manageable and on target. This might involve coaching towards bringing both their work and retirement goals into sharper focus and/or facilitating the coachee to get motivated towards achieving their work and retirement goals. Coachees' agendas can be far ranging and include aspects of their work, personal and retirement life: preparation and planning for retirement; management of work-based and lifestyle issues; time management; personal development; decision-making; exploring options and/or expectations; self-identity; maximising self-confidence; relationships and social life; health; hobbies, leisure and interests; finances; housing; and work in retirement (paid and unpaid).

Common coaching areas also include dealing with retirement in a healthy and positive way, supporting the coachee through change, goal setting and action planning, optimising resources and retirement/life integration. The approach can be used for all long-term goal-setting and it has a relationship with other coaching specialisms. Indeed, one might suggest that any coach working with a coachee on their long-term life goals is potentially entering into the arena of retirement coaching, although we would be unlikely to attach this label to it at the time. As such, retirement coaching can be seen to share similarities with other coaching specialisms such as executive coaching, career coaching, relationship coaching, health coaching, skills coaching and personal/life coaching.

There are also particular limitations associated with this type of coaching and issues relevant to this coachee group that might or might not be specific to retirement as a life-stage transition. For example, the coachee may be in financial crisis, dealing with bereavement issues, experiencing age-related health issues or having difficulty adjusting to retirement. If presented, such issues should be assessed in terms of the applicability of retirement coaching and the extent to which the coachee's needs might be better met outside of the boundaries of coaching, such as within a therapeutic context.

Different potential coachee groups may enter into third-age or retirement coaching at different life transition points. Figure 7.1 provides some examples of these coachee groupings, representing how diverse coaching can be and that it

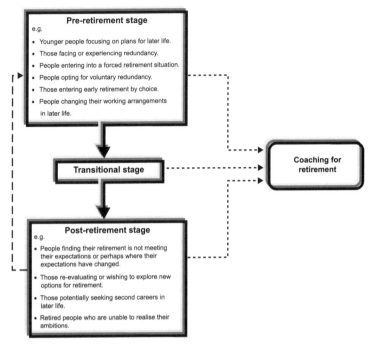

*Figure 7.1* **Coaching retirement as a life-stage transition**

can occur whilst someone is leading up to retirement and both during and after the retirement event. Here we can also see that people range from those who may be focused on their longer-term planning for later life to those who may be finding that currently retirement is not meeting their aspirations.

Where there is particular focus upon strengths, self-continuity and transferable skills, coaching for continuity at earlier life-stage transition points may be important for our quality of later life. For example, theorists suggest that priorities and activities in pre-retirement have greater impact on later life than the actual transition into retirement (Richardson and Kilty, 1991) and evidence also suggests that skills and activities demonstrated by those who adjust success-fully in retirement have been learnt earlier in the lifespan

(Kloep and Hendry, 2007). Approaches based upon positive psychology can be particularly useful when coaching at this life-stage transition point, focusing on motivation, self-identity, supporting people to think in a helpful way about their retirement and facilitation towards behavioural action to achieve goals. Behavioural, cognitive-behavioural and solution-focused coaching work are also approaches that complement this area of practice.

## Case study

Henry[1] was approaching mandatory retirement and as a result of this found that he was coming towards the end of a career working for his current employers operating within the communities sector. This coaching assignment was part of a work-based initiative funded by his employer to support Henry towards a smooth transition into retirement and also to help him work upon his own retirement-related goals. Henry's employers did not request any type of structured or formal feedback either during or at the end of the coaching programme, which was contracted to a maximum of 12 one-hour sessions and to be flexibly structured to best meet Henry's agenda.

The coaching commenced approximately 6 months prior to Henry's mandatory retirement date. As the referral had been made by the employer, the first session was an introductory meeting between coach and coachee to enable a face-to-face conversation around what the coaching relationship might look like and how coaching could best help and support him. Whilst he had a general idea of the purpose of coaching, an early problem encountered was based on his expectations of what coaching could offer him. Having come along with a very open mind, a specific downside of this was his lack of clarity in term of the benefits, boundaries and limitations of coaching. This was discussed and agreed in this first introductory session. The format of all coaching sessions was face to face although there was some communication between sessions via email and the telephone. Any potential boundary issues with the use of modern communication were discussed in the very first meeting.

In the first coaching session an assessment was undertaken and Henry identified some topics that he wished to work on. This ranged from a healthy adjustment to the scaling down of his current work role and responsibilities, managing conflicting work issues in terms of his pending retirement and exploring both personal and work-related post-retirement options. An issue that Henry presented was that his expectations of retirement had been ineffectively reviewed and assessed to date and as such were based on vague plans and 'wants' that were not viewed or framed as goals. This was making it hard for him to know where to start and take action. During the second session there was a further emphasis on assessment in terms of the current situation as well as a move towards action planning. A further goal also emerged at this point in the programme, and as a recurring theme in subsequent sessions, that related to Henry's desire to explore paid work options for his post-retirement. Following sessions enabled Henry and his coach to work on his immediate-, medium- and longer-term planning and action steps. He also began to develop an awareness and understanding of the blocks, both practical and psychological, that were inhibiting his goal attainment. This in turn provided him with insight to develop strategies and take action that challenged these blocks and enabled him to move forward.

Whilst an integrated approach was used, this coaching assignment mainly combined aspects of positive psychology and behavioural and cognitive-behavioural coaching. Early on in the coaching a theme of employment and self-continuity had emerged as Henry set about making plans to continue with some type of work following on from mandatory retirement. As such, drawn from positive psychology, strengths coaching became a useful approach. Action steps included identifying Henry's transferable skills and ways in which he might nurture his current resources. Undertaking research to inform decisions regarding moving home (including downsizing) and possible re-training for a second career were all set as goals during the coaching. Behavioural strategies worked on included time management and communication to support Henry to overcome blocks to moving forward with agreed actions. Activities undertaken between sessions were particularly focused on information-gathering and undertaking research to support him in his decision-making regarding relocating and finding work post-retirement. In some cases cognitive-behavioural techniques were also introduced to motivate Henry and help him to think about his retirement in a helpful way, thus facilitating him to take action.

The outcome of coaching was that Henry explored his options, which resulted in either the goal attainment he was seeking or the reframing of his work and retirement aspirations so that an action plan was developed for now and in the future. He was also able to identify his transferable skills and key resources, which was an important outcome for him as one key concern he had shared was about becoming detached from his network and resources post-retirement. Having researched his options and taken action to seek work post-retirement, Henry was successfully re-employed shortly after leaving his previous full-time career role.

What follows is some coach–coachee dialogue[2] to illustrate retirement coaching in action.

*Coach:*    What would you like to take away from today's coaching session?

*Coachee:*  Following my official retirement date I plan to continue to undertake work of some type. Today, I would like to focus on ways in which I might go about this.

*Coach:*    What steps have you taken so far?

*Coachee:*  I am really just at the thinking stage at the moment. I seem to have lots of options available to me and I am not sure which way to go. For example, I could perhaps find a placement in an area related to my current profession or alternatively re-train and start a second career.

*Coach:*    What has prevented you from moving this thinking forward?

*Coachee:*  I feel a bit stuck at the moment as to what direction to take.

*Coach:*    Because?

| | |
|---|---|
| *Coachee:* | I start to think about it and then I begin to feel a bit overwhelmed. |
| *Coach:* | For you, what is the most overwhelming part of exploring post-retirement work options? |
| *Coachee:* | That I might not be able to find anything out there. |
| *Coach:* | And if you were not able to find anything out there? |
| *Coachee:* | It would mean that I have been left on the scrap heap. |
| *Coach:* | What would you say to a friend or colleague experiencing the same issue? |
| *Coachee:* | I would tell them to take one step at a time . . . Perhaps they need to undertake some research first before putting this kind of pressure on themselves. |
| *Coach:* | Okay, would this be advice that you would follow yourself? |
| *Coachee:* | Yes! It sounds like a straightforward approach and less overwhelming. |
| *Coach:* | What do you need to do to make this happen? |
| *Coachee:* | I could read the local papers to see what job adverts are out there and also talk to friends who I know have been in a similar situation. |
| *Coach:* | Anything else? |
| *Coachee:* | Yes, I can pick up a prospectus from the local college and see what courses they are running at the moment. |
| *Coach:* | What else? |
| *Coachee:* | Basically information-gathering to help inform my next steps. |
| *Coach:* | What other resources or people do you have available to you that can help with this information-gathering? |
| *Coachee:* | I also have a contact who works in an agency and I could have a conversation with them as to the likelihood of me finding a work placement. |
| *Coach:* | Anything else? |
| *Coachee:* | No, I think that is all for now. Although . . . I could also start writing up a list of my useful contacts. |

*Coach:*      We have highlighted a number of options. What are the first steps you can take to help you to move towards your goal of exploring post-retirement work options?

*Coachee:*    I am going to drop an email to my agency contact when I get home today. Also I can pick up a prospectus from the local college when I pass next week and then spend some time researching possible courses I might be interested in taking. Between now and our next session I will start writing up a list of useful contacts within my work and personal network.

*Coach:*      What might stop you from undertaking these actions?

*Coachee:*    Nothing I am aware of sitting here today.

*Coach:*      You mentioned that if you were unable to find anything out there then it would mean that you were on the scrap heap . . .

*Coachee:*    Yes, although saying that out loud has already helped me to see that I have been thinking about my future in rather all-or-nothing terms.

*Coach:*      Are there any other actions you could undertake between now and our next session to check out this belief?

*Coachee:*    To challenge this and keep me motivated it would also be really helpful for me to make notes of my research . . . so I can collate the evidence regarding the possible work opportunities and other options available to me.

## Discussion issues

1  In what way has retirement changed over the last 50 years? What predictions can you make about the way in which it might change in the course of the next 50 years?

2  Outline five main themes from this chapter and critically consider the extent to which they might influence the retirement experience of individuals in modern society.

3   What is the value and contribution of coaching in comparison to other retirement interventions?

## Endnotes

1   Name has been changed and details disguised to protect the
coachee's identity.
2   Based on the case study but not the actual dialogue.

## References

Aaron, H. J. (Ed.) (1999) *Behavioural Dimensions of Retirement
Economics*. Washington, DC: Brookings Institution Press.
Atchley, R. (1988) *Social Forces and Aging* (5th ed.). Belmont, CA:
Wadsworth.
Atchley, R. C. (1976) *The Sociology of Retirement*. New York: Wiley.
Atchley, R. C. (1982a) Retirement as a social institution. *Annual
Review of Sociology, 8*: 263–287.
Atchley, R. C. (1982b) Retirement: Leaving the world of work.
*Annals of the American Academy of Political and Social Science,
464*: 120–131.
Beck, S. H. (1982) Adjustment to and satisfaction with retirement.
*Journal of Gerontology, 37*: 616–624.
Beck, S. H. and Page, J. W. (1988) Involvement in activities and the
psychological well-being of retired men. *Activities, Adaption and
Ageing, 11*: 31–47.
Birren, J. E. (2000) Using the gift of long life: Psychological impli-
cations of the age revolution. In S. H. Qualls and N. Abeles (Eds.),
*Psychology and the Aging Revolution: How we Adapt to Longer
Life* (pp. 11–19). Washington, DC: American Psychological
Association.
Blanchflower, D. G. and Oswald, A. J. (2008) Is well-being U-shaped
over the life cycle? *Social Science and Medicine, 66*: 1733–1749.
Bosse, R., Aldwin C. M., Levenson, M. R. and Workman-Daniels,
K. (1991) How stressful is retirement? Findings from the
Normative Aging Study. *Journal of Gerontology, 46*: 9–14.
Braithwaite, V. A. and Gibson, D. M. (1987) Adjustment to retire-
ment. What we know and what we need to know. *Aging and
Society, 7*: 1–18.
Burtless, G. (1999) An economic view of retirement. In H. J. Aaron
(Ed.), *Behavioural Dimensions of Retirement Economics*
(pp. 7–12). Washington, DC: Brookings Institution Press
Cooper, C. L. (1979) *The Executive Gypsy: The Quality of Managerial
Life*. London: Macmillan Press.

Cumming, E. and Henry, W. E. (1961) *Growing Old*. New York: Basic Books.

Department for Work and Pensions (2009) *Full of Life*. London: DWP. Retrieved from http://research.dwp.gov.uk/ageing-society/fulloflife/ on 16 July 2009.

Diener, E. and Diener, C. (1996) Most people are happy. *Psychological Science, 7*: 181–185.

Elwell, F. and Maltbie-Crannell, A. D. (1981) The impact of role loss upon coping resources and life satisfaction of the elderly. *Journal of Gerontology, 36*: 223–232.

Erikson, E. (1968) *Identity, Youth and Crisis*. New York: Norton.

Fernández-Ballesteros. R. and Capara, M. (2003) Psychology of aging in Europe. *European Psychologist, 8*: 129–130.

Friedmann, E. A. and Havighurst, R. J. (1954) *The Meaning of Work and Retirement*. Chicago, IL: University of Chicago Press.

Havighurst, R. J., Neugarten, B. L. and Tobin, S. S. (1968) Disengagement and patterns of aging. In B. L. Neugarten (Ed.), *Middle Age and Aging* (pp. 161–172). Chicago, IL: University of Chicago Press.

Henkens, K. (1999) Retirement intentions and spousal support: A multi-actor approach. *Journal of Gerontology Series B: Psychological Sciences and Social Sciences, 54*: S63–S73.

Holmes, T. H. and Rahe, R. H. (1967) Social Readjustment Rating Scale. *Journal of Psychosomatic Research, 11*: 213–218.

Kim, K. E. and Moen, P. (2001) Is retirement good or bad for subjective well-being? *Current Directions in Psychological Science, 10*: 83–86.

Kim, K. E. and Moen, P. (2002) Retirement transitions, gender and psychological well-being: A lifecourse, ecological model. *Journal of Gerontology Series B: Psychological Sciences and Social Sciences, 57*: 212–222.

Kloep, M. and Hendry, L. B. (2007) Retirement: A new beginning? *The Psychologist, 20*: 742–745.

Latulippe, D. (1996) *Effective Retirement Age and Duration of Retirement in the Industrial Countries between 1950 and 1990*. Issues in Social Protection Discussion Paper 2. Geneva: ILO.

Levinson, D. J., Darrow, C. N., Klein, E. B., Levinson, M. H. and McKee, B. (1978) *The Seasons in a Man's Life*. New York: Knopf.

Lowenstein, G., Prelec, D. and Weber, R. (1999) What, me worry? A psychological perspective on economic aspects of retirement. In H. J. Aaron (Ed.), *Behavioural Dimensions of Retirement Economics* (pp. 215–246). Washington, DC: Brookings Institution Press.

Lundberg, S. (1999) Family bargaining and retirement behaviour. In H. J. Aaron (Ed.), *Behavioural Dimensions of Retirement*

*Economics* (pp. 253–272). Washington, DC: Brookings Institution Press.

Mayring, P. (2000) Retirement as a crisis or good fortune? Results of a quantitative-qualitative longitudinal study. *Zeitschrift für Gerentologie und Geriatrie, 33*: 124–33.

McGoldrick, A. and Cooper, C. (1988) *Early Retirement*. Aldershot: Gower.

McGoldrick, A. and Cooper, C. L. (1994) Health and aging as factors in the retirement experience. *European Journal of Work and Organizational Psychology, 4*: 1–20.

Moen, P. (1996) A life course perspective on retirement, gender, and well-being. *Journal of Occupational Health Psychology, 1*: 131–144.

Mutran, E. J., Reitzes, D. C. and Fernandez, M. E. (1997) Factors that influence attitudes toward retirement. *Research on Aging, 19*: 251–273.

Nadelson, T. (1969) A survey of the literature on the adjustment of the aged to retirement. *Journal of Geriatric Psychiatry, 3*: 3–20.

Office for National Statistics (2005) *Focus on Older People*. Retrieved from http://www.statistics.gov.uk/downloads/theme_compendia/foop05/OlderPeopleOverview.pdf on 25 November 2008.

Office for National Statistics (2008) *Population Trends No. 134*. Retrieved from http://www.statistics.gov.uk/downloads/theme_population/Population-Trends-134.pdf on 11 December 2008.

Palmore, E. B., Burchett, B. M., Filenbaum, G., George, L. K. and Wallmann, L. M. (1985) *Retirement: Causes and Consequences*. New York: Springer.

Payne, C., Robbins, S. and Dougherty, L. (1991) Goal directedness and older adult adjustment. *Journal of Counselling Psychology, 38*: 302–308.

Richardson, V. and Kilty, K. (1991) Adjustment to retirement, continuity vs. discontinuity. *International Journal of Ageing and Human Development, 33*: 151–169.

Richardson, V. E. (1993) *Retirement Counselling*. New York: Springer.

Rowe, J. W. and Kahn, R. L. (1998) *Successful Aging*. New York: Panteon.

Smith, L. C. and Robbins, S. B. (1989, August) *Goal Instability as a Mediator or Older Adult Adjustment*. Paper presented at the 97th Annual Convention of the American Psychological Association, New Orleans, LA. Cited in S. B. Robbins, C. K. Payne and J. M. Chartrand (1990) Goal instability and later life adjustment. *Journal of Psychology and Ageing, 5*: 447–450.

Szinovacz, M. E., DeViney, S. and Davey, A. (2001) Influences of family obligations and relationships on retirement: Variations by gender, race, and marital status. *Journal of Gerontology Series B: Psychological Sciences and Social Sciences*, 56: S20–S27.

## Recommended reading

Aaron, H. J. (Ed.) (1999) *Behavioural Dimensions of Retirement Economics*. Washington, DC: Brookings Institution Press.

Blanchflower, D. G. and Oswald, A. J. (2008) Is well-being U-shaped over the life cycle? *Social Science and Medicine, 66*: 1733–1749.

Kloep, M. and Hendry, L. B. (2007) Retirement: A new beginning? *The Psychologist, 20*: 742–745.

McGoldrick, A. and Cooper, C. (1988) *Early Retirement*. Aldershot: Gower.

# Part II

## Developmental coaching – themes and applications

# Positive psychology and strengths coaching through transition

## P. Alex Linley, Robert Biswas-Diener and Emma Trenier

*Change is the only constant.*

(Heraclitus, 6th C. BCE)

Whether we like it or not, our lives are continuously punctuated by transitions. The transitions from homecare to school, from school to college, from college to work, from living with parents to living independently, from living free to the responsibilities of parenthood – all are examples of the normative developmental life transitions that many of us will encounter. Allied with these developmental life transitions, we also find ourselves experiencing many transitions in our working lives – career moves, promotions, stretch assignments, restructures, changes in working patterns, locations or colleagues, sometimes redundancy and ultimately retirement. But, as Heraclitus noted over two and a half millennia ago, 'change is the only constant'. Transitions are part of our lives, and they are here to stay (although constantly changing . . .).

Life transitions, whether major or minor, can often be difficult. They tend to require additional psychological resources such as effort, perseverance, optimism and self-efficacy. Transitions are natural, and no-one is immune to them. Transitions vary in both their causes and magnitude. Some transitions are thrust upon us suddenly, as in the case of a car accident victim who is injured; some are

gradual processes that are expected to take time to negotiate and adjust to, such as moving to a new city or taking
a new job; some are continuous, such as ageing; and some
are minor, such as adapting to driving a manual transition
gear when one is accustomed to an automatic. In each case
the concept of 'transition' denotes newness, such as adding
a new piece to one's sense of identity or building a new
skill set.

Although these transformative periods can be stressful,
they can also be invigorating and exciting. Many people
look forward to anticipated rewards that often follow transition periods. Coaching people through these inevitable
changes often means addressing client stresses and anxiety
at the same time as harnessing client excitement. The new
science of positive psychology provides a number of creative,
enjoyable and strengths-focused techniques for coaching
people successfully through transitions, as we go on to
explore.

## The structure of this chapter

In this chapter, we want to do three things. First, we will
introduce you to some of the ways in which positive
psychology – and psychological insights generally – can be
applied to helping people navigate their life's transitions
successfully. Second, we will look specifically at work transitions, particularly around losing one's job through outplacement and redundancy, as an area where our own practice
focuses on coaching people through transition. Third, we
will explore in greater depth the role of strengths coaching
through transitions, as a model of how positive psychology
and the strengths approach are being applied in our work
helping people through transitions. In doing so, we will
introduce the three broad stages to transition coaching that
we typically use, namely *life evaluation*, *strengths identification* and *pathway mapping*. To begin, though, we commence
with an exploration of how some of the key principles and
research insights of positive psychology can be used to
inform transition coaching.

## Who is walking over my bridge?
## The hidden nature of transitions

Just as the troll hides under the bridge in the famous story of the *Billy Goats Gruff*, transition is a bridge spanning periods of life that hides some potential hazards. Transition, by definition, is a period of change from one stage to another, whether those stages are jobs, times of life or changes in health. Transitions, especially major ones, are notoriously difficult. Humans are unique among animals in that our highly developed forebrains allow us the cognitive capacity to think about the future. This ability is something of a blessing and a curse. Because we can consider times to come, we can modify our behaviour to avoid negative consequences, plan for emergencies and sacrifice short-term goals for long-term goals. These abilities give humans a crucial adaptive advantage. But, because the future is not completely certain, it can create stress. Take the example of an entrepreneur who wants to invest in a new technology venture. Gathering data, making careful decisions and having a long-term vision will likely enhance her possibilities of success. However, knowing that the venture is risky and could fail, and clearly understanding what a loss of investment money will mean, could also raise anxiety (Biswas-Diener and Dean, 2007).

It turns out that how we look at the future is one of those trolls lurking under the bridge of transition. Research evidence from a wide range of positive psychology sources suggests that our natural future focus can raise levels of stress, but can be effectively dealt with as well. First, studies reveal that people have a natural tendency to be vigilant for negative outcomes (Baumeister et al., 2001) and are more affected by losses than gains (Slovic, Fischhoff and Lichtenstein, 1982). From an evolutionary standpoint, a little bit of worry, whether it is about our declining health or our new business, is likely to provide the emotional motivation to proceed cautiously and avoid unnecessary risks. This natural phenomenon is compounded by the systematic errors that people make in predicting how we will feel in the future (Gilbert, 2007). In studies of 'affective forecasting', researchers Daniel Gilbert and colleagues (1998) asked participants to predict how they would feel in the future. For example, they asked young faculty members how they might feel if they were granted or denied tenure. While the respondents were able to correctly assess the valence of emotion – that is, they knew that receiving tenure would 'feel good' and being denied tenure would 'feel bad' – they made consistent errors regarding the magnitude and the duration of the emotional impact.

Central to this latter phenomenon is the fact that people often overlook the natural human capacity to adjust to new circumstances and regain their former levels of happiness (Diener, Lucas and Scollon, 2006). While the young academics who did not receive tenure were disappointed, they were neither as 'devastated' as many of them predicted they would be, nor did this negative emotional period last as long as they predicted it would have. Affective forecasting has direct consequences on our decisions. If, for example, a client feels she will not be able to adjust to life overseas because she will feel too lonely, she may turn down an attractive job offer. While, ultimately, there are no right or wrong answers to such decisions, people may forego risk without sufficient basis or consideration of how that risk might be mitigated and ultimately overcome.

---

**Coaching strategy:** When faced with change, decisions and transition, people often consider only the short-term future, because it is the easiest to imagine. It is typical for clients to focus heavily on the stresses related to the transition phase while overlooking the adaptation that will almost certainly follow. Asking clients to describe their lives in 3 months, 6 months or a year after the change period can be helpful in re-focusing their attention on possible positive outcomes. As coaches, we ought to be mindful for our clients that in some cases their fear of transition alone will mean they do not make changes or grasp opportunities that otherwise they well might.

The idea of future-mindedness and risk assessment is particularly interesting in the context of coaching because, as coaches, we often encourage our clients to take risks and push themselves beyond the limits of caution. While we hope to offer the client an opportunity to reflect on the risks, benefits and realism of important life ambitions, we often cheer them on as they approach transitions and encourage them to commit to goals. The idea behind commitment is that it is central to motivation and will help clients to persevere through difficulty (Koo and Fishbach, 2008). This, however, is not always the case. An interesting study by Pomerantz, Saxon and Oishi (2000) shows that the more heavily individuals commit themselves to goals, the more anxiety they can feel. As a coach, it is worth considering how pushing for commitment could affect the client's psychological state. According to Pomerantz and associates, participants who focused heavily on failure and the impact of failure were more likely to worry than those who focused on perceived progress and accomplishment. This suggests that, where coaching clients are concerned, working with them to find effective ways of measuring progress will be more likely to promote positive moods and minimise worry.

The other troll hiding under the bridge of transition periods is 'identity'. A person's identity is central to how they function, relate to those around them and perceive themselves, their capabilities and outlook for the future. Many life transitions are particularly difficult psychologically because they involve integrating new elements into one's identity while shedding outdated self-concepts. As we look across the human lifespan we see a developmental trajectory that includes various life stages (Erikson, 1995). While the precise details of these stages differ by culture, the concept of 'stations of life' such as childhood, mid-life and old age are universal (Shweder, 1999).

Interestingly, as people, including coaching clients, enter new life stages they are vulnerable to stereotypes related to that particular stage. Research by Steele and Aronson (1995) shows that stereotype vulnerability can result in a 'self-fulfilling prophecy' such that people behave in ways consistent with the stereotypes. Women and African-

Americans, for example, who were told that the maths scores of women and African-Americans are typically lower than those of Whites subsequently underperformed on maths tests relative to their gender and race-matched peers who were not given these instructions and hence did not have the same perception of ageing. This is similar to the priming effects found by Bargh, Chen and Burrows (1996) in which people's behaviour was directly affected by subtle primes, with one intriguing study showing that participants walked more slowly when they left the laboratory if they had been primed about stereotypes of old people.

Both of these lines of research underscore the importance of raising the issue of identity with coaching clients. Coaches may be more effective to the extent that they work with clients to explore stereotypes and expectations related to the new period following transition. Recent research on 'positive ageing' is particularly illustrative of this point. In a longitudinal study Levy and colleagues (2002) found that people 50 years and older who had a positive view of their own ageing (e.g. 'Things keep getting better as I get older') were significantly more likely to outlive their negative counterparts, controlling for socio-economic status. Based on this line of research we advocate for the strategic use of mentors and role models who provide illustrations of the positive aspects of ageing and post-transition success.

## Coaching hope

In keeping with the theme of future-mindedness, as discussed earlier, we believe that an important contribution of positive psychology to coaching is the research, theory and assessment of hope. Hope is a psychological tonic that allows individuals to weather tough times and is correlated with a number of desirable outcomes, including better physical health, better psychological adjustment and more positive interpersonal relationships (Rand and Cheavens, 2009). Hope, linguistically interchangeable with optimism, is the belief in a positive future. Snyder's (1994) Hope Theory includes two major facets as people orient towards their goals. First, 'pathways thinking' is associated with higher rates of hope. Pathways thinking is the ability to produce alternative solutions or routes to a desired outcome. In coaching, pathways thinking is often accomplished through brainstorming solutions to problems. The second aspect of Hope Theory is called 'agency thinking'. Simply put, agency thinking is a sense of self-efficacy or self-confidence. People who believe they have more personal control over positive outcomes are higher in hope. For coaches, this theory can be useful because it is simple to learn and easy to understand.

---

**Coaching strategy:** Hope can be used both diagnostically and as a strategic intervention by coaches. Diagnostically, it can help to listen to clients discuss their expectations of the future. Often, clients sound 'hopeless' and in these instances it can be informative to consider which of the two branches of hope the client might be low on. Narrative themes related to a lack of ability or expectations of poor performance can be indicators that the low-hope client has low agency thinking. Low-hope clients who continue to employ failed strategies or do not discuss alternatives are likely to be low in pathways thinking. Identifying which branch to work on can guide coaching interactions towards brainstorming and creativity interventions (to boost pathways thinking) or towards acknowledgement and support interventions (to boost agency thinking).

---

## Coaching through redundancy

Having examined some of the ways in which positive psychology can be used to inform transition coaching generally, we now turn our attention to answering the question: How can positive psychology practitioners present an alternative approach to coaching people through redundancy?

For a start, coaching interventions focused on redundant employees should be seen as only *part* of the solution. This is because it is not only redundant employees who are affected by their redundancy – the remaining employees and the organisation are also affected. At the Centre for Applied Positive Psychology (CAPP) we believe that a whole system approach to outplacement (redundancy support) is required: building the hope, courage, strengths recognition and self-efficacy of redundant employees; building the collective hope, cohesion and vision of remaining teams; and providing managers with the support and skills that they need to positively influence the emotional climate of their teams. We deal next with each of these elements in turn.

### Coaching redundant employees

When coaching redundant employees, timing is everything. What works at one stage of the process of adjusting to change will not work at another. The key is to identify where the individual is in the cycle of responding to change, often termed the 'change curve', and then choose your coaching strategies accordingly.

#### Moving towards negative emotion

When people are given news of their redundancy, common emotional reactions include anger, despair and grief. These emotions need to be recognised and dealt with before the individual will be capable of moving on. This principle can be seen in research into what Stanton and her associates refer to as 'emotion-focused coping' (Stanton et al., 2000), which demonstrates that when people move towards, rather than away from, a stressful encounter (emotional approach) through processing and expressing their emotions they are able to cope with it more successfully. For this reason, coaches need to take an emotionally intelligent approach that offers the client the time, space and permission to reflect and express negative emotion. In doing so, and using more motivational approaches later when the individual is ready to move forward, the individual will be more able to find sustainable happiness.

#### A shift in perspective

How we perceive events determines the way in which we react to them. As Diener, Lucas and Oishi (2002: 68) wrote: 'It appears that the way people perceive the world is much more important to happiness than objective circumstances.' For an individual who has passed through the initial shock of redundancy and is experiencing depression, or grappling to make sense of their situation, coaches can intervene by enabling them to develop a realistic and healthy perspective. At this point, the level and nature of psychological distress experienced by the individual may be influenced by: the attributions that the individual makes about the cause of the redundancy; the degree to which they view the event as a crisis; the importance they have placed on work and wealth as a contributor to their happiness; the level of control they feel over their next steps; and whether they can also see the opportunities that it may bring. Coaches can encourage the growth of resilience, personal agency and motivation by assisting their clients to overcome self-defeating and crisis-escalating perceptions.

---

**Coaching strategy:** Look out for self-defeating and crisis-escalating perceptions and consider helping the client to make the following perspective shifts:

1 *Depersonalisation* – acknowledging that the redundancy is due to a global, economic recession (for example) rather than because of personal or manager fault.

2 *Happiness mosaic* – acknowledging that work and wealth are components of happiness amongst many others such as spirituality, health, family and leisure.

3 *Whole-life narrative* – acknowledging that this is one transition amongst many others that will take place during the natural course of life.

4 *Control* – acknowledging that whilst the redundancy decision was uncontrollable, one's responses to it are controllable.

5 *Gratitude* – accepting that there are some things to be grateful for and considering the opportunities that the redundancy could bring.

## Start with strengths

As the individual accepts their situation and gains the strength to move on, coaching that builds confidence, self-efficacy and optimism will be beneficial. Beginning from an understanding of strengths (see below for further exploration), the individual can consider what the most fulfilling aspects of their future role will be. This strengths-based approach to outplacement differs from traditional support, which tends to focus on applying transferable skills (regardless of whether they are energising to use or not), job search skills and goal-setting. In contrast, by starting with strengths, clients are enabled to identify and focus on what really matters to them, what they enjoy doing and how they want to spend their working time in the future – all of which are valuable bedrock data for under-pinning their future career search and aspirations.

## Coaching teams

Following redundancies, the motivation and commitment of remaining employees tend to falter – as shown by increased absenteeism and turnover and decreased discretionary effort and organisational commitment. So, a strengths-based approach to outplacement will focus attention on remaining teams as well as redundant employees.

Building *collective hope* – the level of goal-directed thinking of a large group of people (Snyder and Feldman, 2000) – and *collective self-efficacy* – 'the extent to which we believe that we can work together effectively to accomplish shared goals' (Stanton et al., 2002: 284) – are tangible ways in which coaches can intervene by using exercises such as the G-POWER model (Pedrotti, Lopez and Krieshok, 2000). Doing so as part of a wider appreciative approach (Cooperrider, 1986) will enable the team to identify the historical, personal and collective strengths of the team and increase their readi-ness for change by visualising and planning for the future.

## Coaching managers

Managers also play a pivotal role. A manager will typically be bearing multiple layers of strain – their own uncertainty, pressure from above and pressure from below. Classic research on arousal (e.g. Schachter and Singer, 1962) suggests that people turn towards their social surroundings to better understand the emotions they are feeling. Other researchers have noted the importance of establishing a positive climate during organisational change, where employees label the turmoil as positive and challenging rather than negative and distressful (Mossholder et al., 2000).

For this reason, positive management behaviour, for example role modelling positive attitudes towards change and embracing an open and transparent communication style, affects the emotional climate of the team for the better. Coaches can help managers to identify their 'problem' or 'redundant' behaviours and counter these with alternative ways of acting. For example, if the manager acknowledges that the 'checking' routines they have always employed are no longer required as outgoing employees get ready to leave, they may counter these with other more appropriate routines such as 'enquiring' or 'supporting'.

---

**Coaching strategy:** When organisations are making redundancies, managers are placed under great strain. For this reason, coaching managers to use their strengths effectively during the period of crisis, to affirm and build their personal resilience and to increase their hope (personal agency and pathways thinking) will benefit them personally and also benefit their teams.

---

## Strengths coaching through transitions

Whatever the type of transition that our clients may be facing, it will almost always throw up the opportunity for them to re-evaluate their lives and the direction they are taking, and to consider whether or not they are using their strengths optimally. Our work on strengths coaching through transitions has some of its roots in our earlier research on post-traumatic growth, which is concerned with how people grow and change positively following difficult life events. Even in the most negative of experiences, people can transform their experience into an ultimately positive developmental outcome, whether through an enhanced sense of wisdom (Linley, 2003) or through a myriad of other positive changes following this enforced, non-normative traumatic transition (Linley and Joseph, 2004). A theme that emerges commonly from these lines of research is that people re-evaluate what is important to them and make life changes accordingly, and also pay much closer attention to what they may be capable of and thus how they are going to spend their time in the future.

As we started to describe above, a substantial amount of our work has been concerned with coaching people through the transition of redundancy, and especially doing so in a way that helps them to identify and harness their strengths more fully in the service of what they want to achieve in the future. This coaching typically proceeds through three broad stages: *life evaluation*, *strengths identification* and *pathway mapping*.

*Life evaluation* is concerned with helping people to assess where they are now against where they might want to be. It is a pause and stock-check of their life to this moment that can be done to a relatively superficial level, or more deeply by exploring themes and trends that may have emerged and evolved through their childhood and beyond. Questions that we might use in this life evaluation phase include:

- What do you remember your life being like as a child?
- What are your significant memories of your early life?
- What stands out for you when you think about your upbringing? How do you think that has affected who you are today?
- Did you have a plan to be doing what you have been doing for the last few years? If not, how did that come to pass?
- Are you doing what you always wanted to do? If not, what have been the things that got in your way?
- If you had a magic wand, what would you be doing with your life going forward from here today?

We typically find that the answers to these questions throw up a series of themes and trends that can be used to orient the person towards what matters to them most and what they want to achieve in the future – a core element of successful transition coaching, since people need to know where they want to be headed and what success looks like if they are going to get there.

*Pathway mapping* follows *strengths identification*, although for reasons of expediency and flow we treat them out of sequence here. Having identified their strengths, we then spend time looking at how the client can use those strengths to enable the desired future that they want to create. There is never a guaranteed one-to-one mapping between the strengths that somebody may possess and what they want to achieve, but rather a myriad of pathways through which a person's strengths could be aligned to the goals that matter to them. It is here where transition coaches working from a strengths perspective can add significant value, by helping the client to work through those different options and permutations of the client's strengths and capabilities and how they can be used in service of the outcomes they want to achieve.

*Strengths identification* sits at the core of our strengths coaching approach to transitions, and rests on identifying and then developing the client's strengths in order to help them navigate their transition journey successfully. There are a number of strengths identification tools available, and transition coaches may have a preference or may use one or more of them in combination (as well as combining them with other assessments of areas such as personality, motivation and values). As we go on to explain below, we use CAPP's leading edge strengths assessment tool, Realise2, but also introduce the other major tools that are available.

Coaches may be increasingly familiar with strengths, given the growth in interest in the field over the last decade. The major strengths tools available include the Clifton StrengthsFinder™ (www.strengthsfinder.com; Clifton and Anderson, 2002; Rath, 2007), the VIA Inventory of Strengths (www.viastrengths.org) developed by Peterson and Seligman (2004) or the Inspirational Leadership Tool (www.inspiredleadership.org.uk) developed by the British DTI (Department of Trade and Industry) and Caret, a management consultancy (see Morris and Garrett, 2010). The Clifton StrengthsFinder™ and the Inspirational Leadership Tool (ILT) use an ipsative approach to assess 34 and 18 strengths, respectively, whereas the VIA Inventory of Strengths (VIA-IS) uses a normative approach to assess 24 character strengths (for the VIA-IS norm data for the UK population, see Linley et al., 2007). Both StrengthsFinder™ and the VIA-IS typically report back one's 'top five' strengths, whereas the ILT reports back on all 18 characteristics. Both the VIA and the ILT are available free of charge online, whereas the StrengthsFinder™ is obtained through an access code available in a number of books written by staff at The Gallup Organization.

## Integrating strengths, learned behaviours and weaknesses: The Realise2 model

As will be apparent from the brief review of strengths tools above, all of them simply report back on one's 'top strengths' in some way, and do so using personality-style assessment methodologies (i.e. asking people to choose between two different statements in an ipsative format, or asking people to rate how much a statement is 'like them' using a normative format). In contrast, CAPP's Realise2 model (www.realise2.com) was developed on a very different and, we would argue, more fitting premise for strengths assessment and development, which also allows the identification of what we refer to as learned behaviours and weaknesses.

Realise2 assesses 60 different attributes according to the three dimensions of energy, performance and use, and then combines the responses for each of these dimensions for any given attribute to determine whether the attribute is a realised strength, an unrealised strength, a learned behaviour or a weakness.

*Realised strengths* are those strengths that you recognise and use regularly – but there can still be surprises here, in that there may be many things we have as strengths but that we do not automatically recognise and accept as such (Kaplan, 1999). *Unrealised strengths* are those strengths that may be lying dormant in us, waiting for the opportunity to arise or for the right situation to call them forth (Lyons and Linley, 2008).

*Learned behaviours* are those activities that we do often and we may be very good at but are not energising for us. Regular learned behaviours can present a real psychological trap that we need to be aware of, since we can do things regularly – and be asked to do them more – because we are good at doing them, yet to do so repeatedly over time would lead to an increasing sense of feeling disenfranchised and disengaged because the critical *energising* component is missing.

*Weaknesses* are exactly as the label suggests – those areas of performance that could be causing you problems. As we go on to explore below, these are the weaknesses that need to be most effectively managed to make them irrelevant. As long as they are kept that way, they can be safely ignored. But if the situation changes and they are pushed into the foreground, the weaknesses will then need to be managed quickly and effectively if performance is not to be undermined – all of which provides fertile ground on which to work for the strengths coach, especially if the areas of weakness for a given client could become exposed through the transition journey they are setting out to navigate.

Realise2 can be completed online in around 20 minutes, and also provides the functionality for users to manage their own development and set up their individual personal development plan for future development activities, both of which have proven a valuable resource for people as they work through transitions.

Depending on the time and resources available, we may also use a strengths identification technique that we call the Individual Strengths Assessment (ISA). This was first described in chapter 4 of Linley (2008), and the interested reader is referred to this source for a fuller description.

The ISA combines the strength-spotting skills of a strengths coach with the tell-tale hallmarks of a strength that can be found through listening for strengths (see Linley, 2008, chapter 4). The ISA involves the strengths coach asking a series of questions, in a semi-structured and free-flowing way, that then allow the person to talk about their strengths in an easy, natural manner as part of a conversation. As this conversation is happening, the strengths coach is noting and identifying the strengths that shine through. The strengths are not typically fed back to the person as they are identified – this would often break the flow of the conversation. Instead, they are noted by the strengths coach, who then seeks additional validation and support for what they have heard, by asking additional follow-up or supporting questions. Towards the end of the conversation, or at another appropriate point, the strengths coach then feeds back what they have heard to the participant.

The beauty of the ISA is that it is not explicitly about your strengths, but rather it gets to explore your strengths through the 'back door' into your consciousness. Consider, for example, some sample ISA questions below that are all designed to encourage people to talk about their great experiences, their enjoyment, their best successes – about who they are, at their core, when they are at their best.

The ISA questions cover each of the emotional, thinking and behavioural aspects of people and range over the past, present and future, always looking for consistent themes that would indicate the presence of a strength – and it is hugely important that each of these aspects is covered:

- What sort of everyday things do you enjoy doing?
- What makes for a really good day for you? Tell me about the best day that you can remember having?
- What would you describe as your most significant accomplishment?
- When you are at your best, what are you doing?
- What gives you the greatest sense of being authentic and who you really are?
- What do you think are the most energising things that you do?
- Where do you gain the most energy from? What sorts of activities?
- What are you doing when you feel at your most invigorated?
- Tell me about a time when you think that 'the real me' is most coming through.
- Do you have a vision for the future? What is it about?
- What are you most looking forward to in the future?

- Thinking about the next week, what will you be doing when you are at your best?

(Adapted from Linley, 2008, chapter 4.)

It is important to recognise that the ISA does not work according to a script. It is, unfortunately, not a foolproof process whereby anyone can read the questions from the list and establish what someone's core strengths are. In contrast, it is a subtle but powerful combination of the questions of the ISA and the expertise of the strengths coach. The ISA questions move people into the right territory to be thinking about their strengths. The coach's own strengths, together with their skill and experience, allow them to draw those strengths out through the conversation, before feeding them back to the client in such a way that the client understands, values and engages with the strengths. All of these questions start to open up the dialogue around strengths, around what energises and invigorates people and what gives them a sense of authenticity, and enables them to be at their best.

It is important to note that, in the case of all these questions, the ISA conversation is just that – a conversation. It is not an interview, or somebody reading from a scripted list of questions. As such, the strengths coach is always at liberty to tailor the questions so that they feel comfortable and they fit within the context and flow of the conversation, as well as the needs and expectations of the client.

As the conversation draws to a natural conclusion – when the responses are all pointing in the same direction, and little new material or indicators are coming through – it is very often helpful to ask people what, on the basis of the conversation, they think their strengths are. This can also be a good opportunity to introduce the question around other feedback that people may have had through formal or informal processes, and whether that feedback is consistent with what they have started to identify through the ISA conversation.

Particularly as one works with a client on transition coaching issues, the ISA can be used as a powerful means of opening up the strengths identification conversation with them to its fullest extent. We will often cross-validate by using both a Realise2 assessment and an ISA, as a means of really exploring in depth what a person's strengths are and the situations in which they may play out. This deep strengths exploration helps the client to internalise and own their strengths much more fully, and in so doing to build them into the self-concept and identity that they will take with them as they work through their transition, as our case example next demonstrates.

## Case study: Life journey and transitions through a Realise2 lens

Working with one client specifically, who we will call Anna, we noted how her learned behaviours all seemed to reflect behaviours and aptitudes that were very much required at a particular earlier life transition, following the untimely death of a parent when our client had to take over the running of the family business. These characteristics had become deeply engrained at this critical developmental juncture, and to an extent had defined her (very successful) career to date in the financial services field, yet it became apparent through the strengths identification phase (by virtue of her Realise2 report and the coaching exploration that preceded this) that these capabilities were not energising and were not where this woman's particular passions lay. She could do them, and do them well (indeed, had done them well for many years and to great effect), yet at this moment of transition, when she was able to pause, take stock and reflect, it slowly became clear that these were not the foundation stones on which she wanted to build her future career.

In contrast, a deeper set of strengths were also identified that Anna found deeply energising and engaging, and it was these to which she wanted to commit her attention and focus, using them as the basis from which to start to define what she was going to strive to achieve in the future. Of course, it is typically early days in the transition when we are engaged as coaches, so seeing the long-term developmental trajectory and outcomes may be rare, but we have every confidence that Anna will go on to many successes that build from her recognition of what she does well and loves to do (her strengths), as distinct from those things she does well but that ultimately drain her (her learned behaviours).

## In conclusion: Positive psychology for positively navigating transitions

In this chapter, we have demonstrated some of the myriad of ways in which positive psychology and strengths approaches can be used by coaches to support their clients through a variety of transitions. We have majored on career transitions, notably redundancy, as being transitions where coaches may be more likely to be involved, and have explored a number of inputs from positive psychology that can support transition coaching, but focusing on our own work on strengths coaching through transitions.

Overall, we hope to have emphasised the case that transitions are inevitably a part of life, and that as such they can be grasped as turning points from which we can re-orient ourselves towards what we really want, and from there to navigate a more fulfilling way forward. To quote an oft-used Latin dictum, we encourage all coaches to inspire their transition coaching clients with the positive affirmation *Carpe Diem* – if we are able to help our clients re-connect with what really matters to them, and work to achieve it through drawing from what they do best and what they love to do, they will be powerfully enabled to seize the day and transform their inevitable transitions into opportunities for fulfilment lasting long into the future.

## Discussion issues

1  What are the core factors that enable clients to deal with transitions positively rather than negatively?
2  How does positive psychology and the strengths approach lend itself to transition coaching? How can you use the principles and practices described in this chapter in your own transition coaching?
3  Where do your clients find greatest leverage from their strengths? How can you help them to harness their

strengths more fully in the pursuit of what they want to achieve, at the same time enabling them to enjoy the journey along the way?

4   As a coach, what would be your dream outcomes for your work with your transition coaching clients? How will you achieve them?

## References

Bargh, J. A., Chen, M. and Burrows, L. (1996) Automaticity of social behaviour: Direct effects of trait construct and stereotype activation on action. *Journal of Personality and Social Psychology*, 71: 230–244.

Baumeister, R. F., Bratslavsky, E., Finkenauer, C. and Vohs, K. D. (2001) Bad is stronger than good. *Review of General Psychology*, 5: 323–370.

Biswas-Diener, R. and Dean, B. (2007) *Positive Psychology Coaching: Putting the Science of Happiness to Work for Your Clients*. Hoboken, NJ: Wiley.

Clifton, D. O. and Anderson, E. C. (2002) *StrengthsQuest: Discover and Develop your Strengths in Academics, Career and Beyond*. Washington, DC: Gallup Press.

Cooperrider, D. L. (1986) *Appreciative Inquiry: Toward a Methodology for Understanding and Enhancing Organizational Innovation*. Cleveland, OH: Case Western Reserve University, University Microfilms International.

Diener, E., Lucas, R. E. and Oishi, S. (2002) Subjective well-being: The science of happiness and life satisfaction. In C. R. Snyder and S. J. Lopez (Eds.), *The Handbook of Positive Psychology* (pp. 63–74). New York: Oxford University Press.

Diener, E., Lucas, R. E. and Scollon, C. N. (2006) Beyond the hedonic treadmill: Revising the adaptation theory of well-being. *American Psychologist*, 61: 305–314.

Erikson, E. (1995) *Childhood and Society* (new ed.). London: Vintage.

Gilbert, D. (2007) *Stumbling on Happiness*. London: HarperPerennial.

Gilbert, D. T., Pinel, E. C., Wilson, T. D., Blumberg, S. J. and Wheatley, T. P. (1998) Immune neglect: A source of durability bias in affective forecasting. *Journal of Personality and Social Psychology*, 75: 617–638.

Kaplan, R. E. (1999) *Internalizing Strengths: An Overlooked Way of Overcoming Weaknesses in Managers*. Greensboro, NC: Center for Creative Leadership.

Koo, M. and Fishbach, A. (2008) Dynamics of self-regulation: How (un)accomplished goals affect motivation. *Journal of Personality and Social Psychology*, 94: 183–195.

Levy, B. R., Slade, M. D., Kunkel, S. R. and Kasl, S. V. (2002) Longevity increased by positive self-perceptions of aging. *Journal of Personality and Social Psychology, 83*: 261–270.

Linley, A. (2008) *Average to A+: Realising Strengths in Yourself and Others*. Coventry, UK: CAPP Press.

Linley, P. A. (2003) Positive adaptation to trauma: Wisdom as both process and outcome. *Journal of Traumatic Stress, 16*: 601–610.

Linley, P. A. and Joseph, S. (2004) Positive change following trauma and adversity: A review. *Journal of Traumatic Stress, 17*: 11–21.

Linley, P. A., Maltby, J., Wood, A. M., Joseph, S., Harrington, S., Peterson, C., et al. (2007). Character strengths in the United Kingdom: The VIA Inventory of Strengths. *Personality and Individual Differences, 43*: 341–351.

Lyons, L. S. and Linley, P. A. (2008) Situational strengths: A strategic approach linking personal capability to corporate success. *Organisations and People, 15*: 4–11.

Morris, D. and Garrett, J. (2010) Strengths: Your leading edge. In P. A. Linley, S. Harrington and N. J. Garcea (Eds.), *Oxford Handbook of Positive Psychology and Work* (pp. 95–105). New York: Oxford University Press.

Mossholder, K. W., Settoon, R. P., Armenakis, A. A. and Harris, S. G. (2000) Emotion during organizational transformations. *Group and Organization Management, 25*: 220–243.

Pedrotti, J. T., Lopez, S. J. and Krieshok, T. (2000) *Making hope happen: A programme for fostering strengths in adolescents*. Unpublished Master's thesis, University of Kansas.

Peterson, C. and Seligman, M. E. P. (2004) *Character Strengths and Virtues: A Handbook and Classification*. New York: Oxford University Press.

Pomerantz, E. M., Saxon, J. L. and Oishi, S. (2000) The psychological trade-offs of goal investment. *Journal of Personality and Social Psychology, 79*: 617–630.

Rand, K. L. and Cheavens, J. S. (2009). Hope theory. In S. J. Lopez and C. R. Snyder (Eds.), *Oxford Handbook of Positive Psychology* (pp. 323–333). New York: Oxford University Press.

Rath, T. (2007) *StrengthsFinder 2.0*. New York: Gallup Press.

Schachter, S. and Singer, J. (1962) Cognitive, social and physiological determinants of emotional state. *Psychological Review, 69*: 379–399.

Shweder, R. A. (1999) Culture and development in our postcultural age. In A. S. Masten (Ed.), *Cultural Processes in Child Development* (pp. 137–148). Mahwah, NJ: Lawrence Erlbaum Associates, Inc.

Slovic, P., Fischhoff, B. and Lichtenstein, S. (1982) Response mode, framing, and information-processing effects in risk assessment. In R. M. Hogarth (Ed.), *New Directions for Methodology of Social and Behavioral Science: The Framing of Questions and the*

*Consistency of Responses* (pp. 21–36). San Francisco, CA: Jossey-Bass.

Snyder, C. R. (1994) *The Psychology of Hope: You Can Get There From Here*. New York: Free Press.

Snyder, C. R. and Feldman, D. (2000) Hope for the many: An empowering social agenda. In C. R. Snyder (Ed.), *Handbook of Hope: Theory, Measures and Applications* (pp. 389–412). San Diego, CA: Academic Press.

Stanton, A. L., Kirk, S. B., Cameron, C. L. and Danoff-Burg, S. (2000) Coping through emotional approach: Scale construction and validation. *Journal of Personality and Social Psychology, 66*: 350–362.

Stanton, A. L., Danoff-Burg, S., Cameron, C. L., Bishop, M., Collins, C. A., Kirk, S. B., et al. (2002) Self-efficacy: The power of believing you can. In C. R. Snyder and S. J. Lopez (Eds.), *Handbook of Positive Psychology* (pp. 277–287). New York: Oxford University Press.

Steele, C. M. and Aronson, J. (1995) Stereotype threat and the intellectual test performance of African Americans. *Journal of Personality and Social Psychology, 69*: 797–811.

## Recommended reading

Biswas-Diener, R. and Dean, B. (2007) *Positive Psychology Coaching: Putting the Science of Happiness to Work for Your Clients*. Hoboken, NJ: Wiley.

Gilbert, D. (2007) *Stumbling on Happiness*. London: HarperPerennial.

Linley, A. (2008) *Average to A+: Realising Strengths in Yourself and Others*. Coventry, UK: CAPP Press.

Snyder, C. R. (1994) *The Psychology of Hope: You Can Get There From Here*. New York: Free Press.

# Managing generations

## *Ben Green and Helen Williams*

In this chapter we consider the differences in attitudes, values and behaviours of the four generational cohorts that exist in today's workforce, with reference to the impact on the organisation and on managerial practice. Although authors differ in exact years that define the four generations, they are widely classified and described (Howe and Strauss, 2007; Smola and Sutton, 2002; Stauffer, 2003) as follows:

- **Veterans**. Born before 1948, these workers experienced the Second World War in their childhoods and are often characterised as conventional and risk averse (Howe and Strauss, 2007). They currently make up around 11% of the UK workforce (Allen, 2008).
- **Baby Boomers**. Born between 1948 and 1963, this generation joined the workforce at a time of high competition, and successful careers are often judged as being earned through hard work (CIPD, 2008a). This generation currently makes up around 30% of the UK workforce (Allen, 2008).
- **Generation X**. Born between 1964 and 1978, Generation X grew up at a time of great diversity, insecurity and rapid change (Smola and Sutton, 2002). This led to Generation X often being considered as rather individualistic (Jurkiewicz and Brown, 1998) and greatly used to change and uncertainty (Kupperschmidt, 2000). Currently, Generation X makes up around 32% of the UK workforce (Allen, 2008).
- **Generation Y**. Also known as Millennials, these individuals were born between 1979 and 1994. The internet,

supportive parenting and economic growth are amongst the factors to have shaped their outlook (Guthridge, Komm and Lawson, 2008). Generation Y currently makes up around 27% of the UK workforce (Allen, 2008).

This chapter will examine the interrelations between these four generations in today's organisations and present considerations at both the organisational and individual management levels.

## Considerations for organisations

The workplace in which members of Generation Y have begun their careers is a very different environment to that in which the generational cohorts before them started their working lives. As a result of globalisation and huge advances in information and communication technology, and in order to respond rapidly to changing environments and markets, organisation structures have become leaner, more flexible and network based (Overholt, 1997; Symon, 2000). In today's organisation, management layers have been flattened and outsourcing of non-core business activity has become widespread in order to enable fast decisions and eliminate unwanted bureaucracy (Symon, 2000). Traditional, hierarchical structures in which Veterans and Baby Boomers were used to operating are less familiar to Generation X and more recently Generation Y, who have become used to flat hierarchies, dispersed working environments and complex reporting structures (CIPD, 2008a).

The co-existence of four generations in this modern workplace therefore creates a number of considerations and challenges for an organisation to be aware of in order to ensure that its generationally diverse workforce can work together effectively and harmoniously.

### *Technology*

Generation Y, and to a lesser extent Generation X, have grown up throughout the 'Information Age' (Sheahan, 2009a; Deloitte, 2009) where information is readily at hand, most

notably through the internet and mobile devices such as tele-
phones and Personal Digital Assistants (PDAs). Contrast
this with Veterans and Baby Boomers, who grew up with
radio and the beginning of television as their main media,
and it is easy to see how expectations of the utility of communicative technologies can vary across the generations at
work. While older workers are likely to see, and benefit from,
more instantaneous communication with their colleagues,
younger employees will expect increasingly advanced and
varied ways of staying connected with their co-workers
(Sheahan, 2009a). Central to this is the development of
Web 2.0 technology, which allows internet users more scope
to generate content (e.g. Blogs, Podcasts and Wikis) as well
as to filter and keep up to date with information from multiple
sources (e.g. Real Simple Syndication[1]). As more companies
embrace these technologies (see McKinsey Quarterly Survey,
2008) they should be aware that they might deter Veteran
and Baby Boomers, and therefore appropriate training and
support should be provided (CIPD, 2008a).

Many authors and surveys have commented on the fact
that Generation Y employees see the boundaries between
work and social life as blurred (CIPD, 2008a; Pollack, 2008).
Although they value work–life balance, they are more
inclined than generations before them to actively seek out
workplaces where they can have fun and socialise with
colleagues in and out of work time (Sheahan, 2009b).
However, the growth of Web 2.0 technologies has meant that
this connection with colleagues may take place online, via
social networking sites and instant messaging. Today's
organisation, therefore, would benefit from bearing this
factor in mind when considering policies for the use of
communication technologies amongst its staff (Martin,
Reddington and Kneafsey, 2008). The organisation might
also consider how best to use these technologies in the
attraction and retention of new employees (CIPD, 2008b;
Martin et al., 2008), a consideration that will be addressed
later in this chapter.

The ease with which information can be accessed from
sources such as the internet and the multitude of television
stations now available also has implications for the ways in

which rules, processes and cultural norms are set out in organisations. As various commentators point out, Generation Y employees will not be afraid to challenge workplace regulations such as clothing policies and schedules, as they are acutely more aware of how things work at other organisations (Allen, 2008; NAS Insights Survey, 2006).

## *Home and flexible working*

Improved information and communication technology has made today's workplace a more connected environment, as well as a more flexible one. Employees working from home, either on a permanent or occasional basis, have become increasingly prevalent in organisations (Lepir, 2002) and a recent survey revealed that two-thirds of UK employees expect to be able to work from home within the next 5–10 years (Affiniti Survey, 2007).

This method of working has been facilitated by remote access to Virtual Private Networks (VPNs) over broadband internet connections, and the rising popularity of handheld email devices such as the BlackBerry™. Organisational advantages of such practices come in the form of reduced requirement for expensive overheads such as office space, as well as less reliance on the talent pool of employees located near to their premises. For the employee, advantages come in terms of broadening options of employment without having to relocate, and having the ability to be more flexible regarding home commitments such as families. However, the characteristics of the four different generations currently existing in the workplace affect not only the way these individuals benefit from more flexible working practices, but also how flexible working practices should be structured in order to gain the maximum benefit for the organisation.

Starting with the Veterans, there exists an opportunity for organisations to retain the skills and knowledge of this experienced group through alternative contracts, such as part-time or contract-based employment (CIPD, 2008a). The *Gen Up* report by the CIPD in the UK has also shown that a high proportion of Veterans would consider working beyond retirement if they could choose the hours they worked (CIPD, 2008a). Baby Boomers, on the other hand, are less inclined to consider working beyond retirement age, although flexible working opportunities feature high in their decision-making process when joining an organisation. Baby Boomers also report less inclination to be motivated by team-work in their role, which may make them more open to the less overtly social nature of remote working (CIPD, 2008a).

Generation X employees will value flexibility in their jobs in order to fit well into their life outside of work, and many would be prepared to work longer hours if flexibility was offered (CIPD, 2008a). Generation X employees also tend to value outcome over process and will therefore enjoy flexibility that decreases the time spent in what they view as unnecessary meetings. They are also more likely to ask 'What's in it for me?' with regard to work tasks (Smola and Sutton, 2002). Generation Y employees, who are towards the start of their careers, value work–life balance but are also prepared to put in extended working hours in order to gain employability (CIPD, 2008a). They will tend to look to achieve this by choosing an employer where they can be part of a team, have fun and make friends with their colleagues (Deloitte, 2009; Sheahan, 2009b). This generation is inher-ently comfortable with the technologies that facilitate remote working, but also desire cooperation with colleagues and face-to-face time with others at work (CIPD, 2008a; Deloitte, 2009).

## *FreshMinds – connecting to Generation Y at the heart of the business model*

FreshMinds (www.freshminds.co.uk) was founded in 2000 with the aspiration of becoming the world's most respected research and recruitment consultancy. Today, the organisa-tion runs three separate business units, FreshMinds Research, FreshMinds Talent and FreshNetworks, all of which display the unique characteristics of the networked nature of Generation Y.

*FreshMinds Research* provides organisations with inspired thinking and analysis that helps them understand their customers, competitors and markets, while *FreshMinds*

*Talent* works with companies to source executive, graduate and interim talent. At the heart of both of these businesses is an innovative flexible working model based on the concept of 'Minds'. Since its inception, the company has built a team of over 16,000 Minds – a network of analysts, consultants and researchers throughout Europe, ranging from talented undergraduate students through to independent subject matter experts and professionals. Minds work with FreshMinds Research to fulfil briefs for clients and also make up the candidate pool that FreshMinds Talent draws on to find outstanding executives, graduates and interim consultants.

Key to this model is the connected and flexible way of working favoured by the Generation Y individuals, who make up the bulk of this group. Location, time and resource constraints on research assignments are overcome by drawing on a diverse pool of highly talented individuals who value the opportunity to structure work around other commitments and further their knowledge and networks.

*FreshNetworks* (www.freshnetworks.com) builds and manages online communities for brands, using interactive techniques developed by the connected Generation Y. By building these communities and social networks online, FreshNetworks gives its clients a destination for their customers to share experiences, give feedback on the brand and voice positive word-of-mouth online. The FreshNetworks model builds on the trend for customers to engage with like-minded people online, either about brands directly or the lifestyles that they serve. Examples include working with the vitamins manufacturer Vitabiotics to engage customers in the debate around beauty and anti-ageing, and engaging with directors on behalf of BT to collaboratively discuss new products.

FreshMinds' pioneering approach has won them many clients in the private and public sectors and seen them recognised as the industry's 'Most Innovative Employer' at the 2006 Research Excellence and Effectiveness Awards. It is the only agency to have won the Market Research Society's 'Best Agency' Award 2 years in a row.

## Organisational management roles

Today's leaner, dispersed and knowledge-based organisations have also seen changes in the structure and role profiles of management that will affect the different generational cohorts in different ways. As Symon (2000) points out, organisational boundaries have become 'more permeable' and employees form teams and networks to most effectively deal with the problem at hand, rather than having to follow strict organisational channels and hierarchies that characterised companies previously. At first we might consider that Generation Y employees would find this structure a natural way of working, given their comfort with communicative technologies and social networking. However, when we consider that Generation Y are also commonly characterised by a strong desire for support, feedback and encouragement (Healy, 2008; Lancaster and Stillman, 2002; Stauffer, 2003), it becomes clear that organisations will need to also fulfil these needs via the appropriate management structures. Authors such as Howe and Strauss (2007) argue that businesses will need to achieve this by building a more ordered work environment with clearer lines of supervision in order for Generation Y to thrive.

At the other end of the generational ladder, organisations will need to bear in mind the Veterans and Baby Boomers, who, although having accepted the more networked matrix nature of their modern workplace, may be more comfortable with a more hierarchical, chain-of-command structure (Roy, 2008). Furthermore, the older generations will be keen to share their knowledge and experience (CIPD, 2008a) but may find this more difficult to channel without direct reporting lines.

Organisations need to find ways to structure themselves whereby support can be offered to employees at the same time as recognising the often highly complex networked design that the organisation follows. In order to do this, organisations have increasingly started to offer various support networks for employees, ranging in levels of formality from 'Buddy' schemes to more formalised 'mentor' or 'coach' roles (Starcevich and Friend, 1999; Williams, 2006).

These roles are generally characterised by a more person or job focus, rather than the results or productivity focus that might characterise the basis of the supervisor or manager role (Starcevich and Friend, 1999).

Buddy schemes, where new recruits are provided with an informal contact for support, usually at a similar level in the organisation and often with a similar background, have become particularly popular in graduate recruitment (Williams, 2006). Mentoring and coaching programmes might or might not be more formalised in the organisation, and are designed to enhance individuals' development and organisational knowledge transfer (Starcevich and Friend, 1999).

As Keller (2008) points out, members of Generation Y are entering the workforce expecting a collaborative culture that facilitates learning, and various support systems such as buddies and mentors are likely to aid their ambitions to succeed and progress quickly.

## *Talent management*

'Talent management' is an umbrella term for the attraction, development, deployment and retention of talented employees (CIPD, 2006), and has become a strategic priority for organisations in recent years (Guthridge, Komm and Lawson, 2006, 2008). Much of this activity can be attributed at least in part to a seminal piece of McKinsey Quarterly research (Michaels, Handfield-Jones and Axelrod, 2001). This paper suggested that the impending retirement of the Baby Boomer generation would leave organisations competing for the critical shortage of talented employees at senior executive levels. The authors asserted that in order for organisations to succeed in what they termed 'The War for Talent', it was necessary to make talent management a key corporate priority. In order to then recruit and retain the right individuals, Michaels and his colleagues highlighted that the organisation must create and refine a unique value proposition. Above all, this proposition has the objective of convincing potential employees that the organisation offers them incentives, working practices and other advantages that surpass those available elsewhere (Michaels et al., 2001).

Another key tenet of effective talent management is the ability of organisations to develop individuals internally in order to fill leadership positions at all levels throughout the company (Cappelli, 2008). As authors such as Charan, Drotter and Noel (2001) point out, the large number of organisations that feel the need to recruit 'star' leaders suggests that internal succession planning and development have not been at the level they need to be. If organisations are to build their internal leadership capability, therefore, they need to create a value proposition that will also appeal to existing employees in order to improve performance and retention (Peacock, 2008).

As a result of this drive by organisations to become more attractive employers in the eyes of existing and potential staff, more focus and activity has recently been given to employer branding (HR Focus, 2009). Falling under the responsibility of various business divisions, including Human Resources, Marketing and Public Relations, employer branding focuses on informing people about the merits of working for, or with, the organisation (Pinkess, 2008). A challenge arises, however, when organisations define one proposition within their brand in order to appeal to multiple demographics (Guthridge et al., 2008). In order to build a brand that will be attractive to the different generations, organisations are increasingly adapting their offerings and their talent management methodologies to target the different characteristics, values and expectations of these groups (Guthridge et al., 2008; Tucker, Kao and Verma, 2005).

## Attracting and recruiting talent

One of the clearest ways in which organisations have adapted their approach to attract and recruit talent from different generations is in the channel of communication, and in particular the use of technology. Organisations' websites are now generally considered to be a primary means to communicate the message that the company will be a good place to work (Estis, 2008). However, in order to communicate with Generation Y in particular, organisations are increasingly making greater use of Web 2.0 technologies in their recruitment practices (Furness, 2008; Hasson, 2007). Hasson (2007), for example, details how a number of organisations have been successfully utilising recruitment blogs in order to connect with potential employees and provide an 'element of humanity' (p. 66) to the recruitment process. Social networking sites and online communities allow organisations to take this connection even further, by creating groups where interested candidates can interact with existing employees and find information tailored to their requirements (Furness, 2008).

At the other end of the generational spectrum, Guthridge and associates (2008) cite an interesting example of one of the large UK supermarkets, the country's largest employer of over-50s. This organisation's recruitment teams target locations where senior citizens will congregate socially in order to explain the benefits they offer as an employer that are likely to be attractive to this population, including leave for grandparents and caregivers (Guthridge et al., 2008).

As well as tailoring the method of communication to the different generations, companies also need to consider the content of the value proposition they promote to attract different age groups. Although research has found that some aspects are core to a generic value proposition across generations, such as job security and a competitive deal (CIPD, 2008a), there are generational differences in values, attitudes and behaviours around which organisations can tailor their employment brand (HR Focus, 2009). Some of the key preferences of the four generational cohorts are presented in Table 9.1 (based on CIPD, 2008a).

## Developing and retaining talent

As well as tailoring their value proposition to attract and recruit staff, organisations need also to consider how they can respond to the different generational needs and aspirations in order to retain and develop talented individuals.

One of the first considerations worth bearing in mind is how well the organisation actually lives up to the value proposition it puts forward to the different generations. As

*Table 9.1* **Organisational preferences of the four generations (data from CIPD, 2008a)**

| Veterans | Baby Boomers | Generation X | Generation Y |
|---|---|---|---|
| • Emphasis on feeling valued by those around them<br>• Opportunities to coach, support and advise others<br>• Clarity with regard to roles, responsibilities and hierarchies<br>• Reciprocation of loyalty | • Authority to make decisions<br>• Engaged by access to personal development<br>• Corporate Social Responsibility (CSR)<br>• Work–life balance<br>• Less inclined to desire teamwork opportunities | • Authority to make decisions<br>• Flat organisational hierarchies<br>• Flexibility of job to fit in with life outside work<br>• Concern with outcome over process<br>• Value workplaces with a sense of community<br>• Value shorter-term benefits and rewards | • Seek to be part of a team, have fun and make friends<br>• Value challenging work<br>• Desire to attain work–life balance and employability at the same time<br>• Value shorter-term benefits and rewards<br>• Value personal development opportunities in order to grow |

Brandon (2005) points out, presenting an unrealistic picture of the organisation or misrepresenting what employees should expect can be a costly mistake and will often lead to short-lived employee tenure. This assertion also relates to the idea of the 'psychological contract' between employee and organisation (Rousseau, 1996). This concept states that the initial recruitment process will include a number of initial statements that, no matter how imprecise, will give rise to expectations on both sides. If these are not fulfilled by the employer a breach of this psychological contract may be perceived, which may give rise to reduced loyalty and commitment on the part of the employee (Rousseau, 1996).

Assuming that an organisation delivers on the promises it makes when attracting and recruiting staff, it will still need to engage and develop staff in order to retain them and get the most out of them (Sujansky, 2007). Table 9.1 has shown us that the different generations will look for different drivers when it comes to engagement, development and motivation, and it is therefore unlikely that a one-size-fits-all approach will be appropriate. Effective managers will need to vary their style to get the most from employees of different generations (Aker, 2009; Kupperschmidt, 2000), a consideration that will be covered in greater detail later in this chapter. However, there are some overarching considerations in the literature for the organisation to be aware of in formulating development and retention strategies.

First, appropriate reward and recognition schemes need to be put in place in order to appeal to the requirements of the different generations. Generation Y employees entering and progressing through the workplace value regular feedback on their performance (Howe and Strauss, 2007; Sheahan, 2009b; Sujansky, 2002) and organisations will benefit from facilitating this process for managers. Recent research by PriceWaterhouseCoopers (PWC) has also shown that Generation Y employees will tend to value training and development as benefits, over and above remuneration (PWC, 2008), highlighting an interesting consideration for organisations structuring benefits packages.

The organisation should also recognise that career paths need to be clear and accessible for employees, particularly for Generations X and Y, who value diverse job opportunities and possibilities for international and lateral career paths (Sheahan, 2009b). The PWC research cited previously has shown that the popular belief that Generation Y employees are willing to move at will between employers might not be the full picture (PWC, 2008, cited by Dawe, 2008). Instead, the research suggests that this generation expect to be employed by between just two to five companies in their lifetime, but do demand high quality training and development and international opportunities. Organisations that can offer these prospects to employees therefore have every chance of retaining them (PWC, 2008).

A third consideration for the organisation in terms of retaining and developing staff of different generations is in how knowledge is shared and transferred between employees. Mentoring and coaching are two methods that are highlighted by numerous commentators as being important in this respect (Ruch, 2005; Starcevich and Friend, 1999). Organisations are likely to benefit by ensuring that mentors and coaches are not reserved solely for the more senior executives (PWC, 2008) as well as considering the reversal of roles, so that more senior employees can benefit from the skills that the younger generations have to offer (Greenes and Pitkialis, 2008, cited in Wagner, 2008; Ruch, 2005).

## *External considerations*

The UK's Employment Equality (Age) Regulations, set out in 2006, make it unlawful to discriminate, directly or indirectly, against workers, employees, job seekers and trainees because of their age (Acas, 2006). Therefore, although organisations will benefit from developing value propositions that will appeal to the different generations, they need to ensure that these do not discriminate on the basis of age. For example, limiting recruitment activity solely to university campuses for graduate posts is likely to be indirect discrimination, as it would severely restrict the chances of older graduates applying for the post (Acas, 2006). Similarly, the use of technology, such as Web 2.0, in recruitment and training may provide barriers to entry for certain age groups participating and therefore lead to discrimination.

The regulations do not mean that organisations cannot tailor approaches and solutions to different generations, but do mean that they need to be aware of possible discrimination and ideally take positive action in order to avoid this (Acas, 2006). For example, organisations should ensure that they know the age profile of employees in order to plan for retirement peaks and take action to rectify age imbalances (Acas, 2006). Staff surveys and exit interviews will also allow organisations to monitor the views of different age groups and plan remedial action for any issues.

## Considerations for managers

This chapter has so far outlined a number of considerations for organisations to be aware of in terms of making a success of a multi-generational workforce, within the bounds of regulations regarding age discrimination. The remainder of the chapter will focus on generational differences from the perspective of a manager with a multi-generational team. In this respect, we aim to raise awareness of possible sources of opportunity and conflict within such a team, as well as to suggest some practical management considerations in order to leverage skills and experiences across the generations. As we have seen earlier in the chapter, today's organisational structures often lead to a number of informal and formal management roles that can often be temporary and formed for a specific task or purpose. The perspectives that follow are therefore intended not just for individuals with a remit as formal line managers, but in fact any individual who might take responsibility for the completion of a task through a team.

### *Communicating with the different generations*

The cross-generational manager is likely to need to use different communication methods to different effect for the varying ages of employees in his or her team (Pitkialis, 2009). The highly connected Generations X and Y, who are used to being able to access information freely, often prefer 'sound-bite' communications delivered in a just-in-time manner (Eiser, 2009). Their Baby Boomer and Veteran colleagues, however, are more likely to be assured by fuller accounts of situations and prefer communication to follow appropriate channels in the organisation (Pitkialis, 2009). The CIPD *Gen Up* report (2008a) also points out that the generations will vary in the extent to which they feel the need to trust communications, with Generation X feeling this to be more important than Baby Boomers and Generation Y. Managers may therefore need to bear this in mind when delivering sensitive or uncertain messages to Generation X team members.

As Hammill (2005) points out, at the start of any team formation, an effective leader will benefit from spending time learning how the team members wish to communicate, particularly if that team is cross-generational in nature. This can include the form of communication, as outlined above, but will also relate to frequency, timing and style of communication (Hammill, 2005). Various conflicts may arise in the team as a result of not taking these factors into account (CIPD, 2008a; Kupperschmidt, 2000). For example, Generations X and Y are widely regarded as valuing work–life balance as more important than do their Baby Boomer counterparts (CIPD, 2008a; Guthridge et al., 2008; Howe and Strauss, 2007). A telephone call from a colleague regarding work that is received outside of working hours may therefore be received differently by individuals from different generations. As another example, an effective leader will vary his method of instruction to complete a task for different generations. Veterans are likely to be used to a more directive style of communication, whereas Generations X and Y are likely to challenge commands and prefer a more collegial and participatory approach to the task (Hammill, 2005; Howe and Strauss, 2007).

## Engaging and motivating the different generations

We have seen earlier in the chapter that in order to win the 'War for Talent' (Michaels et al., 2001), organisations will need to offer varying value propositions that tap into the characteristics of the different generations. Only by doing this will they be able to attract talented individuals and keep them engaged and committed to the organisation. In terms of how this affects the cross-generational manager, we need to consider factors both intrinsic and extrinsic to the work being undertaken, as well as the different types of commitment that might be evidenced by the different generations (CIPD, 2008a; Guthridge et al., 2008; Meyer and Allen, 1991).

From an extrinsic point of view, an effective manager will look to create the correct work environment for the different generations. Factors such as communication within the team, as outlined previously, will undoubtedly have a bearing on this. Also relevant for the manager's attention will be the sense of workplace community offered and the flexibility of working arrangements. An effective manager will recognise that Generations X and Y's desire for flexible working practices does not necessarily indicate a desire to work fewer hours (CIPD, 2008a). The manager should also recognise that Veterans and Baby Boomers may be more attuned to 'presenteeism' (CIPD, 2008a: 18) in the office as an indicator of hard work.

The intrinsic nature of the work that employees are carrying out will also be an important consideration for the cross-generational manager. For example, one of the observed characteristics of Generation Y employees is that they will seek meaning in their work more than the generations before them (Guthridge et al., 2008). This means that they will value fairness and ethical behaviour, but will also be keen to understand how their contribution affects the bottom line for the organisation (NAS Insights Survey, 2006). Generations X and Y strive for efficiency and innovation in their work much more than the generations before them (Howe and Strauss, 2007). Challenging tasks are also extremely important to these individuals, but in order to feel engaged they will need to know that they have the resources available to them to get the work done (CIPD, 2008a).

The cross-generational manager will also benefit from an awareness of different forms of organisational commitment when considering individuals' engagement and motivations to stay with the organisation. Meyer and Allen's (1991) model of organisational commitment proposes three components that characterise an employee's commitment to the organisation – affective commitment, continuance commitment and normative commitment – as illustrated in Table 9.2. Affective commitment across all generations might be due in part to the right employer brand or value proposition, but managers should consider how this can be enhanced in different individuals in their teams. By their very nature, the other two components of Meyer and Allen's (1991) model may vary across age groups and generations. For example, it is clear that a Veteran or Baby Boomer who has been with an organisation for many years is likely to have stronger feelings of continuance commitment than a Generation X or Generation Y employee, particularly if they have commitments such as a

*Table 9.2* **Meyer and Allen's three-component model of organisational commitment (data from Meyer and Allen, 1991)**

| Commitment component | Definition |
| --- | --- |
| Affective commitment | An employee's emotional attachment to, identification with and involvement in the organisation. Employees with a strong affective commitment continue employment with the organisation because they *want* to |
| Continuance commitment | An awareness of the costs associated with leaving the organisation. Employees whose primary link to the organisation is based on continuance commitment remain because they *need* to do so |
| Normative commitment | A feeling of obligation to continue employment. Employees with a high level of normative commitment feel that they *ought* to remain with the organisation |

pension scheme. A younger Generation Y employee, on the other hand, might report stronger feelings of normative commitment due to the organisation offering them their first job and investing in their training. Understanding these forces will help the multi-generational manager to retain and engage employees.

At the time of writing this chapter, the global economic downturn has meant that many Generation Y employees are seeing the effects of recession and instability for the first time. How these individuals cope with such an economy remains to be seen. Some warn that Generation Y's tendency to live for the present, coupled with large student debts, could lead to them being hit particularly hard (Lim, 2008). However, optimism comes from the fact that the incentives craved by Generation Y, such as recognition and feedback, come without a price and are therefore a benefit in a cost-conscious economy (George, 2009). Furthermore, a recent study by Randstad, cited by Laff (2008), indicated that, despite their desire for work–life balance, Generation Y employees showed more commitment and desire to put in additional effort in difficult times in comparison with their colleagues from the other generational cohorts.

## Managing performance, recognising and rewarding

A large number of authors have commented on Generation Y's requirement for regular feedback on their performance, particularly in comparison with previous generations (Howe and Strauss, 2007; Sheahan, 2009b; Sujansky, 2002). Many authors, such as Eiser (2009), attribute this to heavy parental involvement in their upbringing, with a focus on goals and more structured extracurricular activities, which are often team-oriented and emphasise achievement. Cross-generational managers should, therefore, expect to provide feedback on a more frequent basis to their younger team members than they might be used to; waiting until the end-of-year appraisal is unlikely to be appealing to Generation Y (Sheahan, 2009b). Managers should look to exploit the technology and communication methods that Generation Y favours in order to help them provide this feedback efficiently. It is likely that managers will have more scope to deliver additional informal feedback to this generation, as these individuals are more likely to place their manager in their network of social contacts (CIPD, 2008a).

If it is within their jurisdiction to do so, managers of Generation Y employees, as well as Generation X, should consider shorter-term reward and recognition strategies (Sheahan, 2009b; Wilkinson, 2007). As Sheahan (2009b: 2) observes, these employees 'prefer a small reward now, rather than the promise of a big reward later'. The older generations of Veterans and Baby Boomers, on the other hand, will be more used to the concept of putting in the years of service for a reward at the end and may espouse a message of 'one day this could all be yours' (Sheahan, 2009b: 2). Individuals from the Veteran and Baby Boomer generations will be particularly keen to be recognised and valued by those around them, by being able to share their opinions, knowledge and experience with more junior employees (CIPD, 2008a). Managers would benefit from using coaching and mentoring schemes, as discussed earlier in this chapter, in order to recognise older generations' experience whilst also satisfying the appetite for learning of the younger generations.

Stauffer (2003) presents a succinct summary of goal-setting and performance management, focusing on the key characteristics of the four generations. He points out that key to motivating Veterans are explanations of the logic behind actions, formality over informality and use of traditional forms of recognition such as plaques and certificates. Baby Boomers will, according to Stauffer, be motivated by a clear series of steps towards a defined goal. Recognition that is widely noticed, such as an article in the company newsletter, is likely to motivate these individuals. In setting goals for Generation X, Stauffer argues that the manager should tell them what needs to be done but not how to do it, allowing them to set their own priorities and providing frequent and frank feedback. Recognition in the form of bonus days off will appeal to their desire for work–life balance. Finally, Stauffer points out that Generation Y's work goals should be set based on an understanding of these individuals' personal goals and recognition of the interplay between the two. Communication, as highlighted earlier in this chapter, should be regular and informal.

## *Managing knowledge transfer and capitalising on generational strengths*

The successful cross-generational manager is likely to be the individual who can structure and manage the team to make the most of the skills, behaviours and experiences of the team members (Kupperschmidt, 2000; Ruch, 2005). However, in order to aid the development of the individuals in that team, it should be ensured that knowledge is being transferred between team members. This can be provided 'top down' by mentoring opportunities, as highlighted earlier in this chapter, but as authors such as Greenes and Pitkialis (2008) point out, this knowledge transfer should be a two-way process – that is, the younger members of the team can usefully provide fresh insights and technological know-how to their more experienced colleagues. This knowledge transfer should be carried out in a way that facilitates the learning styles of the different generations (Greenes and Pitkialis, 2008), bearing in mind the effectiveness of various media for information transfer (Murray and Peyrefitte, 2007).

Finally, as Gratton and Erickson (2007) point out, the complex tasks facing today's organisations almost always require the input and expertise of people with disparate views and backgrounds in order to provide insight and innovation. However, these authors also point out that collaboration in such teams can often be hampered by perceived differences between team members, a point that is supported by social psychology theories arguing that similarity is a potent factor in affiliation and collaboration (Festinger, 1954). Furthermore, the virtual team environments that are often demanded from today's global organisations can also lead to a decline in collaboration (Gratton and Erickson, 2007). In order to maximise the success of such teams, Gratton and Erickson argue that the manager or leader will need to role-model collaborative behaviour, take both a task and relationship orientation and support a sense of community in the team.

## Summary

This chapter has summarised some of the key attributes, styles and behaviours of the four generations that co-exist in today's workplace. Some of the major impacts of these different generations have been considered, both at the organisational level and at the level of the individual manager or leader. These considerations have also been referenced in relation to the UK's Employment Equality (Age) Regulations (2006).

Individual differences in ways of working, engagement and motivation do of course pervade each generation, and therefore it is unwise for the organisation or manager to make sweeping generalisations concerning employees based solely on their generational cohort. However, the abundance of research and discussion papers in this area illustrates a number of marked differences in attitudes and working styles between the generations, resulting from a variety of economic, social and technological changes. In order to ensure future success, organisations will benefit from considering these in the attraction and management of talented staff.

## Discussion issues

1   What differences do you see in the behaviours, attitudes and values of individuals from different generations in your organisation?
2   Which generations does your organisation's employer brand connect with most effectively? What are the advantages and disadvantages of this?
3   How much scope is there for managers in your organisation to be flexible with rewards, benefits and feedback for employees of different generations?
4   In addition to workplace regulations on age discrimination, what other external factors may influence generational considerations?

## Endnote

1   Real Simple Syndication (RSS) is a format designed for sharing headlines and other web-based content. It provides a simple way to keep up to date with rapidly changing content such as news and blog entries (Martin et al., 2008).

## References

Acas (2006) *Age and the Workplace: Putting the Employment Equality (Age) Regulations 2006 into Practice*. Retrieved from http://www.acas.org.uk on 7 February 2009.

Affiniti Survey (2007) MarketWatch. *Technology*, *6*: 16–17.

Aker, J. M. (2009) Managing a multigenerational workforce. *Buildings*, *1*: 46–48.

Allen, A. (2008) Redefining the rules of the generation game. *People Management*, September: 12–13. Retrieved from http://www.people management.co.uk/pm/articles/2008/09/redefining-the-rules-of-the-generation-game.htm on 21 February 2009.

Brandon, C. (2005) Truth in recruitment branding. *HR Magazine*, *50*(11): 89–96.

Cappelli, P. (2008) Talent management for the twenty-first century. *Harvard Business Review*, *86*: 74–81.

Charan, R., Drotter, S. and Noel, J. (2001) *The Leadership Pipeline: How to Build the Leadership Powered Company*. San Francisco, CA: Jossey-Bass.

CIPD (Chartered Institute of Personnel and Development) (2006) Talent management: Understanding the dimensions. *Change Agenda*. London: CIPD. Retrieved from http://www.cipd.co.uk/onlineinfodocuments on 21 February 2009.

CIPD (2008a) *Gen Up: How the Four Generations Work*. London: CIPD. Retrieved from http://www.cipd.co.uk/onlineinfodocuments on 10 January 2009.

CIPD (2008b) *Recruitment, Retention and Turnover Report*. London: CIPD. Retrieved from http://www.cipd.co.uk/onlineinfodocuments on 21 February 2009.

Dawe, T. (2008, December) *What Generation Y Wants from Work*. London: The Times. Retrieved from http://business.timesonline.co.uk/tol/business/related_reports/business_solutions/article 5325378.ece on 7 March 2009.

Deloitte (2009) *Connecting Across the Generations in the Workplace*. New York: Deloitte. Retrieved from http://www.deloitte.com on 21 February 2009.

Eiser, B. (2009) Managing the Millennials. *Pennsylvania CPA Journal*, *80*: 1–2.

Estis, R. (2008) Brand-building basics. *HR Focus*, July: 2.

Festinger, L. (1954) A theory of social comparison processes. *Human Relations*, 7: 117–140.

Furness, V. (2008) Employers go digital. *Personnel Today Guide to Employer Branding*, January: 43–44.

George, L. (2009) Dude, where's my job? *Maclean's*, *122*: 48–49.

Gratton, L. and Erickson, T. J. (2007) 8 ways to build collaborative teams. *Harvard Business Review*, *85*: 100–109.

Greenes, K. and Pitkialis, D. (2008) *Bridging the Gaps: How to Transfer Knowledge in Today's Multigenerational Workplace*. Retrieved from http://www.conference-board.org on 7 February 2009.

Guthridge, M., Komm, A. B. and Lawson, E. (2006) The people problem in talent management. *McKinsey Quarterly*, *2*: 6–8.

Guthridge, M. Komm, A. B. and Lawson, E. (2008) Making talent a strategic priority. *McKinsey Quarterly*, *1*: 49–58.

Hammill, G. (2005) Mixing and managing four generations of employees. *FDU Magazine Online*, Winter/Spring. Retrieved from http://www.fdu.edu/newspubs/magazine/05ws/generations.htm on 16 January 2010.

Hasson, J. (2007) Blogging for talent. *HR Magazine*, *52*(10): 65–68.

Healy, R. (2008) *10 Ways Generation Y Will Change the Workplace*. Retrieved from http://employeeevolution.com/archives/2008/05/

23/10-ways-generation-y-will-change-the-workplace/ on 1 March 2009.

Howe, N. and Strauss, W. (2007) The next 20 years: How customer and workforce attitudes will evolve. *Harvard Business Review*, *85*: 41–52.

HR Focus (2009) Employer and company brands may help competition for top talent. *HR Focus*, *86*: 9.

Jurkiewicz, C. E. and Brown, R. G. (1998) Gen Xers vs. Boomers vs. Matures: Generational comparisons of public employee motivation. *Review of Public Personnel Administration*, *18*: 18–37.

Keller, R. (2008) Make the most of mentoring. *Journal of Accountancy*, *206*: 76–80.

Kupperschmidt, B. R. (2000) Multigeneration employees: Strategies for effective management. *Health Care Manager*, *19*: 65–76.

Laff, M. (2008) Gen Y proves loyalty in economic downturn. *T+D*, *62*: 18. Retrieved from http://www.allbusiness.com/population-demographics/demographic-groups-generation-y/11729793-1.html on 21 February 2009.

Lancaster, L. C. and Stillman, D. (2002) *When Generations Collide*. New York: HarperCollins.

Lepir, J. (2002) Making home work fun. *Global Cosmetic Industry*, *170*: 75.

Lim, J. (2008) Downturn set to hit Gen Y hard. *Money Management*, *22*: 4.

Martin, G., Reddington, M. and Kneafsey, M. B. (2008, July) *Web 2.0: A Discussion Paper. CIPD Research Insight*. London: CIPD. Retrieved from http://www.cipd.co.uk/onlineinfodocuments on 21 February 2009.

McKinsey Quarterly Survey (2008, July) *Building the Web 2.0 Enterprise*. Retrieved from http://www.mckinseyquarterly.com on 21 February 2009.

Meyer, J. P. and Allen, N. J. (1991) A three-component conceptualization of organizational commitment. *Human Resource Management Review*, *1*: 61–89.

Michaels, E., Handfield-Jones, H. and Axelrod, B. (2001) *The War for Talent*. Boston, MA: Harvard Business School Press.

Murray, S. R. and Peyrefitte, J. (2007) Knowledge type and communication media choice in the knowledge transfer process. *Journal of Managerial Issues*, *19*: 111–133.

NAS Insights Survey (2006) *Generation Y: The Millenials; Ready or Not, Here they Come*. Cleveland, OH: NAS Recruitment Communications. Retrieved from http://www.nasrecruitment.com/TalentTips/nasInsights.html on 4 November 2008.

Overholt, M. H. (1997) Flexible organizations: Using organizational design as a competitive advantage. *Human Resource Planning*, *20*: 22–32.

Peacock, L. (2008) The employee is always right. *Personnel Today Guide to Employer Branding*, June: 47–50.

Pinkess, A. (2008) Show you really care to win staff. *Brand Strategy*, July: 38–39.

Pitkialis, D. (2009) Cited in Aker, J. M. Managing a multigenerational workforce. *Buildings*, *1*: 46–48.

Pollack, L. (2008) *Why Your Company Needs Millennials: 5 Reasons to Love Gen Y Workers*. Retrieved from http://www.fastcompany.com on 7 February 2009.

PWC (PriceWaterhouseCoopers) (2008) *Millennials at Work: Perspectives from a New Generation*. Retrieved from http://www.pwc.com on 28 March 2009.

Rousseau, D. M. (1996) *Psychological Contracts in Organizations: Understanding Written and Unwritten Agreements*. Newbury Park, CA: Sage.

Roy, J. (2008) Working with different generations. *Healthcare Executive*, July/August: 7.

Ruch, W. (2005) Full engagement. *Leadership Excellence*, *22*: 11.

Sheahan, P. (2009a) *The Connected Generation*. Retrieved from http://www.petersheahan.com on 12 February 2009.

Sheahan, P. (2009b) *Understand Generation Y*. Retrieved from http://www.petersheahan.com on 12 February 2009.

Smola, K. W. and Sutton, C. D. (2002) Generational differences: Revisiting generational work values for the new millennium. *Journal of Organizational Behavior*, *23*: 363–382.

Starcevich, M. and Friend, F. (1999) Effective mentoring relationships from the mentee's perspective. *Workforce Supplement*, *78*: 2–3.

Stauffer, D. (2003) Motivating across generations. *Harvard Management Update*, *8*(3): 3–6.

Sujansky, J. G. (2002) The critical care and feeding of Generation Y. *Workforce*, May: 15.

Sujansky, J. G. (2007) Make your corporate grass the greenest: 16 cost-effective ways to a culture that keeps your keepers. *Journal for Quality and Participation*, *30*: 9–12.

Symon, G. (2000) Information and communication technologies and the network organization: A critical analysis. *Journal of Occupational and Organizational Psychology*, *73*: 389–414.

Tucker, E., Kao, T. and Verma, N. (2005) Next-generation talent management: Insights on how workforce trends are changing the face of talent management. *Business Credit*, July/August: 20–27.

Wagner, C. G. (2008) When mentors and mentees switch roles. *The Futurist*, January/February: 6–7.

Wilkinson, A. (2007) Future benefits planning must meet the needs of all generations. *Employee Benefits*, July: 5.

Williams, N. (2006, June) Spotlight on ... Buddy schemes. *Personnel Today*. Retrieved from http://www.personneltoday. com/articles/2006/06/06/35767/spotlight-on.-buddy-schemes.html on 12 February 2009.

## Recommended reading

Acas (2006) *Age and the Workplace: Putting the Employment Equality (Age) Regulations 2006 into Practice* (http://www.acas. org.uk).
CIPD (Chartered Institute of Personnel and Development) (2008) *Gen Up: How the Four Generations Work*. London: CIPD.
Howe, N. and Strauss, W. (2007) The next 20 years: How customer and workforce attitudes will evolve. *Harvard Business Review*, *85*: 41–52.
Lancaster, L. C. and Stillman, D. (2002) *When Generations Collide*. New York: HarperCollins.

# Final reflections

## *Sheila Panchal and Stephen Palmer*

The editing of this book has been a fascinating learning experience for us, and it has been a privilege to learn about the inspiring work of our authors and bring together some themes and ideas that connect their work. There are a number of final thoughts that we would like to share.

From Traditionalists to Generation Alpha, we are all on a journey. Throughout the highlights and tough times we continue to learn and grow. In many ways this book is about reflecting on and shaping life stories. As coaches we have a unique opportunity to make a significant and lasting difference to people's lives. We can help people to choose positive and purposeful paths and, through this work, have the chance to influence society more broadly. We therefore have a responsible role, and one final thought is a reminder to all of us to ensure that we are respecting appropriate ethics and boundaries in our coaching work through supervision and other support. As coaches it is fundamental that we understand the scope and limits of our skills. With developmental coaching in particular, the interface with psychotherapy may be blurred and worth keeping in mind.

As coaches and coaching psychologists, our own personal experiences of transitions may be in mind when working with our coachees. Alternatively, we may have no personal experience of a particular transition but this need not prevent us from assisting our coachees. Awareness of potential stereotypes and assumptions about particular ages, stages, transitions and socio-cultural influences is important for coaches. Further exploration of these issues in terms of the coaching relationship is needed, and again supervision plays a key role. Given the key theme of expectations influencing the experience of transitions, this is also an important topic to explore with the coachee. This topic lends itself to the question of advising versus asking and the challenges in maintaining a non-directive approach rather than sharing our own experiences of a transition. Yet, time-limited coach self-disclosure on how they coped with a particular difficulty or transition may help the coachee to see light at the end of the tunnel and move forward. The question of mentor versus coach is important here – others refer to the value of role models and mentors during transitional times (e.g. Garvey, Levinson).

Human development is complex and multi-dimensional, and within this book we have only managed to skim the surface of some of the theories and approaches that can be used to understand it.

The rate of change in our society is phenomenal. We know that the world will be very different for future generations but it is hard to predict how. Some of the generational perspectives discussed in this book will date. For example, at the time of writing we are in the midst of a global economic downturn. However, the overall message remains the same for coaches – to keep the 'bigger picture' in mind. Consider the wider social context within which the coachee experience is embedded, and also bear in mind the principles of human development that remain constant, such as questions of identity and purpose. Levinson acknowledges that human development will depend upon societal and cultural influences, but, drawing upon analysis of biographies spanning many centuries, posits that '. . . the basic nature and timing of life structure development are given in the life cycle . . .' (Levinson, 1986: 11).

Some transitions have been well researched, such as mid-life and retirement, but others less so, such as 'turning 30' and childhood transitions. In addition, a further area for research is lifespan transitions across cultures. Expectations, rituals, values and experiences may differ widely. The discussion in this book has largely focused on the trends and themes present in Western cultures. We look forward to exploring transitions across cultures in the future.

Another final thought is somewhat more pragmatic. How accessible are coaching services to those seeking help with life's turning points? Organisational and executive coaching is one area discussed in this book. Often the 'presenting' coaching issue is more skills or performance related, rather than developmental, yet underlying life transition concerns may be affecting the individual. As such, a developmental perspective can be useful for executive coaches. At other times, organisations may explicitly employ coaching to address transitional issues, such as maternity coaching (Chapter 6). Other methods include working within the institution or system, such as the schools coaching example discussed in Chapter 2. Therefore, individuals may access this type of coaching via schools, other educational establishments, organisations or the services of a personal coach. Further exploration of these access points would be of merit, and to ask how the coaching profession could ensure that their services reach a broader range of people in society who may be facing challenges of dealing with childhood, teenage, early adulthood, mid-life or later life transitions. Also, what channels are available? For younger generations in particular, can we make more use of technology and online channels? How can we work with allied disciplines, such as therapists, financial planners, health professionals and relationship counsellors, to improve access to coaching services? How can we best help?

Systemic perspectives are of relevance. A major facet of this book is a consideration of the bigger picture and context. Issues include working with a school, working with managers, teams and individuals in the context of redundancy and working with managers as well as women in supporting maternity. Keep in mind that people's transitions are experienced by themselves but also have an impact on others. How do lifespan transitions affect relationships, and what does that mean for us as coaches?

The point of intervention is an interesting issue. The discussion in this book lends itself to the view that transitions are linked, and skills and knowledge are transferred from one transitional time to another. Does that suggest, then, that the earlier the intervention into an individual's lifespan the better? Does a greater focus on helping to build resilience in children help them make the most of mid-life? Do individuals assume a certain sequence of transitions, and what is the impact if an alternative sequence plays out?

There is a wider social impact to consider. As the first wave of Baby Boomers turn 65 many Western governments face the challenge of how to finance the national debt and also care for their ageing population. One partial solution being considered by some governments is changing pension benefits and raising the retirement age. Although developmental coaching cannot address this directly it can prepare people to deal with the difficult transitions. One option is that pre-retirement coaching could start as we commence our careers and not just before we retire. Or perhaps all developmental coaching across the lifespan could be seen as pre-retirement coaching, in that questions of purpose and identity are being asked and coping skills are being developed that help people to deal with transitions (see discussion in Chapter 7).

With the older population retiring later, it may re-assert itself more stridently as a source of wisdom in the workplace. We note that Carl Campbell, an artistic director and dance choreographer, asserts that older people whom he calls 're-cycled teenagers' 'have a lot to offer society' (Campbell, 2010).

For many people, as they approach the end-game, i.e. death, just staying alive can become a challenge as health fails. Erikson's maturity phase which focuses on ego integrity vs. despair highlights the difficult path that older people may need to navigate. Most transitions involve loss of some kind, so it is important for coaches to make space for and acknowledge inevitable negative emotions as well as encouraging positive perspectives. With the human capacity to see the worst (affective forecasting), do we help our coachees see a positive past, present and future or hold realistic expectations about transitions (neither crisis nor transformation)?

We hope that this book offers you some useful insights and is the catalyst for further debate and research.

## References

Campbell, C. (2010) Recycled teenagers. Retrieved from http://www.ccdc7.co.uk/recycled-index.htm on 9 September 2010.
Levinson, D. J. (1986) A conception of adult development. *American Psychologist*, *41*: 3–13.

# Web resources

- **Association for Coaching**
  An established professional body.
  www.associationforcoaching.com

- **Association for Professional Executive Coaching and Supervision**
  A professional body specialising in executive coaching.
  www.apecs.org

- **Center on Aging, Health and Humanities, The George Washington University Medical Center**
  Coordinates and conducts research on ageing.
  www.gwumc.edu/cahh/

- **Centre for Applied Positive Psychology**
  Provides positive psychology resources and training.
  www.realise2.com
  www.cappeu.com

- **Centre for Coaching**
  Provides developmental coaching and runs accredited coaching courses.
  www.centreforcoaching.com

- **Coaching at Work**
  Bi-monthly magazine that publishes articles on a range of coaching subjects associated with the workplace. Online resources and articles.
  www.coaching-at-work.com

- **Coaching and Mentoring Relationship Research**
Maintains a list of coach–coachee and mentor–mentee publications that are relevant to this book.
www.coachingrelationshipresearch.webs.com

- **Coaching Psychology Unit, City University London, UK**
Undertakes coaching and coaching psychology research.
www.city.ac.uj/psychology/research/CoachPsych/CoachPsych.html

- **Developmental Coaching Online Resource Centre**
Maintains a list of developmental and transitional coaching publications, information about training and other resources.
www.developmentalcoaching.webs.com

- **European Network for Positive Psychology**
A group of European researchers and practitioners with shared interests in the science and practice of positive psychology.
www.enpp.eu/

- **International Coach Federation**
A professional coaching body with a link to Code of Ethics.
www.coachfederation.org

- **International Positive Psychology Association**
Promotes the science and practice of positive psychology.
www.ippanetwork.org

- **Life-Take2**
Provides tools for addressing the second life-cycle.
www.life-take2.com

- **Mumsnet**
Comprehensive online resource for parents.
www.mumsnet.com/

- **New Zealand Association of Positive Psychology**
  Promotes the science and practice of positive psychology.
  www.nzapp.co.nz

- **Recycled Teenagers**
  Group runs workshops for older people.
  www.ccdc7.co.uk/recycled-index.htm

- **Society for Coaching Psychology**
  A professional body for coaching psychologists with a
  link to Code of Ethics.
  www.societyforcoachingpsychology.net/

- **Society for Intercultural Education, Training and Research**
  SIETAR is the world's largest interdisciplinary network
  for professionals working in the intercultural field.
  www.sietar-europa.org

# Index

*Please note:* Page entries in *italic* refer to figures and tables.